The Adventures of Freckles

Life Lessons from a Mischievous Son of Canada

Autobiographical Sketches
by
Dr. Gordon Guild

World rights reserved. This book or any portion thereof may not be copied or reproduced in any form or manner whatever, except as provided by law, without the written permission of the publisher, except by a reviewer who may quote brief passages in a review.

The author assumes full responsibility for the accuracy of all facts and quotations as cited in this book. The opinions expressed in this book are the author's personal views and interpretations, and do not necessarily reflect those of the publisher.

This book is provided with the understanding that the publisher is not engaged in giving spiritual, legal, medical, or other professional advice. If authoritative advice is needed, the reader should seek the counsel of a competent professional.

Copyright © 2023 Gordon Guild
Copyright © 2023 TEACH Services, Inc.
ISBN-13: 978-1-4796-1729-6 (Paperback)
ISBN-13: 978-1-4796-1730-2 (ePub)
Library of Congress Control Number: 2023912143

All scripture quotations, unless otherwise indicated, are taken from the New King James Version®. Copyright © 1982 by Thomas Nelson. Used by permission. All rights reserved.

Scripture quotations marked KJV are taken from the King James Version. Public Domain.

Scripture quotations marked ESV are taken from The Holy Bible, English Standard Version. ESV® Text Edition: 2016. Copyright © 2001 by Crossway Bibles, a publishing ministry of Good News Publishers.

Scripture quotations marked NIV are taken from the Holy Bible, New International Version®, NIV® Copyright ©1973, 1978, 1984, 2011 by Biblica, Inc.® Used by permission. All rights reserved worldwide.

Scripture quotations marked NASB 1995 are taken from the New American Standard Bible®, Copyright © 1960, 1971, 1977, 1995 by The Lockman Foundation. All rights reserved.

In memory of two special people in my life.

To LeRoy, my older brother, protector, and spiritual guide in my young life. He was chaplain for the Corona, California, police and fire departments. At age sixty-two he met his tragic and sudden end when struck in his car by a truck.

To David, our eight-year-old son, who was struck down on his bicycle by a truck driver under the influence of alcohol. His severe head injury left him in the silent world of a coma for fifteen years until his death. David loved my stories and his Jesus.

LeRoy and David are sleeping now, awaiting the soon-to-come resurrection call to life eternal.

Dedication

To my wife Carol—my best friend, lover, and mother of our four children. Fifty-eight years of loving support and being my "prayer warrior" at home and in the mission fields. My success in life is due to your God centered, quiet, encouraging, and gentle demeanor. I love you the mostest. —Freckles

Table of Contents

Preface	ix
Introduction	11
Do Angels Drive Cars?	12
The Two-Year-Old Runaway	15
Sabbath Baths and Hot Rocks	17
The Christmas Beggar's Present	20
Buster's Broomstick Dilemma	22
Scalloped Potatoes and Macaroni and Cheese	24
Buster and the Car Ride	26
Ocean Bark	27
Saved by the Baby Buggy	29
Fire in the Toy Box	31
Fifty Bee Stings	33
Twenty Percent for Jesus, Eighty for Me!	36
The Disappearing Purse	38
A Bittersweet Lesson	41
The First Canadian Female Astronaut	44
Two Boys and a Bushel Basket of Tomatoes	46

The Nickel Car Key	49
Buster And the Potato Salad	52
The Lost Pocket Knife	54
The Bicycle Siren and a Hamburger Face	56
Winter Wilderness Adventures	58
Frozen Tongue	64
Uncle Tom and a Banana Split	66
A Handful of Blood (and a Fainting Brother)	68
The Bakery Cat	70
Squawking Chickens and Screaming Girls	72
Seven Rivers and a Drowned Volkswagen	75
Hospital Adventures and a Ouija Board	80
A Doctor's Gift and a Broken Hand	83
Frozen Legs: The Mountain Motorcycle Ride	85
The Missing Motorcycle	87
Poisoned	89
The Cherry Bomb Blast in a Dorm Hall!	91
Graveyard Engagement	93
Snake Stories	96
A Heaven-Bound Astronaut (The Day Is Coming!)	100
Gordon's Gin	103
Her Thirteenth Child	105
David and the Rattlesnake	107
Tattoos and Red Roses	109

Unseen Hands	111
A Noise in the Mountain Trees	112
Free Fall Fiasco (Almost)	114
The Disappearing Snowmobile	117
No Brakes and the Bull Moose (and Other Northern Adventures)	119
The Slipping Ladder	123
Mongolian Hospice House Call	125
Bleeding, Bleeding, Bleeding	127
A German Shepherd Puppy Opens Closed Government Doors in Mongolia	130
Do Angels Carry Suitcases? Mission in Moldova	132
Miracle Worker	136
Siberia Mission Adventure	139

Preface

Heart-warming, inspirational, and guaranteed to put a smile on your face, *The Adventures of Freckles* is a collection of stories from the life of a master storyteller. Dr. Gordon Guild's ability to hold audiences spellbound with his fascinating stories shines through in this very personal volume.

From lessons learned from his childhood in Canada to his ongoing experience as a volunteer mission worker, these will grow your faith in the loving God whom Gordon is so well-acquainted with. With true stories of angry bees, chickens in a dormitory, a graveyard marriage proposal (you've gotta read this one!), miracle healings and more, *The Adventures of Freckles* may well become one of your family's favorite collections.

Because this book is often moving and always thought-provoking, you'll be sorry when you reach the end. But then, you can always read it again!

John Bradshaw, President, It Is Written

Introduction

I was born in Vancouver, British Columbia, and raised in many different locations in that province. My father was a professional boxer in his younger years; my mother a housewife and nursing assistant. I had a brother, LeRoy, five years older than me, and twin brothers, Jim and John, five years younger. My sister Chloe was born between my older brother and myself, but she did not survive the trauma of birth. I am looking forward to meeting her in heaven.

After serving in the Royal Canadian Air Force as a wireless gunner operator during World War II, my father became a butcher. He would tell us stories of cattle with large tumors, and how they would cut out the tumors and then send the meat on. It wasn't long before he changed professions, and our family moved toward vegetarianism. No wonder.

As you can imagine, with four rambunctious boys, my mother had her hands full of excitement; some good and some not so good. But she always gave us lots of love. We were poor, but that just made life all the more interesting—and challenging.

I was a blue-eyed, blonde little boy with a mischievous smile and twinkle in my eye. I soon grew reddish, dark brown curls and thousands of freckles; so many that I was nicknamed, "Freckles."

I have been commissioned by my grandchildren, wife, and other family members to write down my life's adventures, which they have enjoyed hearing about many times over the years. Finally, in my eighties, I have taken them up on it, getting these stories down in print before they vanish with me into the silence and rest of the grave.

So enjoy the Canadian kid Freckles and his stories. Who knows? Just maybe you will be able to relate to some of his adventures, from childhood through his medical missionary work around the globe. Relate to them and be spiritually blessed as well. That, at least, is my prayer for this book.

—Freckles, the Canadian Kid

Do Angels Drive Cars?

Everyone's story—everyone's life—starts somewhere, and all our stories touch those of others. In my case, it feels appropriate to begin with a tale from one of the most important people in my life; someone who helped foster my love for God, family, adventure, and storytelling. I was a ten-year-old boy when my dad related this astonishing and true tale to me.

In the 1950s in British Columbia, the relationship between the "white man" and the "Canadian Indians" was not always pleasant. The Canadian Indians* wanted their own land so that they could hunt, fish, and continue their lifestyle. The Canadian government gave land to the Indians in the form of reservations, and whites were not supposed to enter uninvited, especially at night. To do so could prove disastrous.

My dad was trucking lumber from up in the mountains, and the only mountain road was down through the reservation to the local lumber yard, where the rough lumber could be made into boards for buildings. He had talked to the chief and obtained permission to travel through the reservation, but only in the daytime. If caught on the reservation after dark, his life could be in jeopardy. That was the rule.

It was late afternoon, and my dad was hauling the last load of lumber through the reservation. The truck suddenly broke down. He got out his tools but was unable to fix the problem. And he had another problem: it was getting dark quickly. The sun was setting behind the mountains.

What should he do? It wasn't safe to stay in the truck, and he had no way of calling for help. Cell phones and CB radios were not invented yet (only smoke signals). All he could do was walk down the mountain road and hope to get out of the reservation without any Indians seeing him.

---

*"Canadian Indian" or "Indian" were preferred, non-derogatory terms used by indigenous peoples at the time of the story. They remain common today (in addition to "Inuit," which refers to native peoples living further north in Canada). Terminology fluctuates, so out of caution, respect, and for clarity, these most-common terms are used.

It was pitch dark. Every little noise in the trees sounded like Indians coming for him. There were many wild animals in the mountains, too: bears, mountain lions, wolves, and other, smaller critters. The noises, as the wind moved through the trees, were very creepy. He imagined himself either being attacked by a wild animal or being shot by an Indian arrow.

> *What should he do? It wasn't safe to stay in the truck, and he had no way of calling for help.*

Then he heard a car. Who would be driving in the dark on the reservation? Indians did not have cars but only horses and wagons. It sounded like a Model A Ford (it has a unique sound that you don't forget).

My dad was now really scared. *Should I jump in the bushes and hide, or should I keep walking?* he thought to himself.

He prayed for God's protection and felt that he should keep walking. Soon, car lights showed up, as the car pulled alongside my dad and stopped. The driver opened the passenger front door and asked, "Would you two men like a ride?"

"Yes, sir," my dad replied, and jumped in the front seat.

The driver said, "Your buddy can jump in the back." My dad said that it was his truck back up the mountain road that had broken down and that he was alone. The driver said, "Oh, no, I saw two of you walking down the road together." My dad tried to reassure him that he was alone. The man just shook his head and resumed driving.

He asked my dad where he lived and said that he would take him home. Soon out of the reservation and away from danger, they headed to my dad's house. The driver pulled up next to the front yard fence and stopped the car. My dad got out and thanked him, "so much," for bringing him safely out of the Indian reservation. He stood by the fence and watched the car drive down the road, and as it turned the corner—it just disappeared! Vanished into darkness and silence!

My dad stood in wonderment. He never saw the driver or the Model A again.

ॐ∽ॐ∽ॐ∽ॐ∽ॐ∽

I have three questions:
First, who provided the Model A?
Second, who was the driver of Model A?
Third, who was walking with my dad in the dark?
The Bible tells us, "The angel of the Lord encampeth round about them that fear him, and delivereth them" (Ps. 34:7, KJV).

Boys and girls, do you know that Jesus has provided a special angel just for you? That's right. When you say your morning and evening prayers, be sure to thank Jesus for your guardian angel. My dad was certain that his angel helped him that night. It is so nice to trust in the Lord for protection.

The Two-Year-Old Runaway

When I was about two and a half years old, my parents were renting a residential house on about one acre of land. The property sloped down toward the local roadway, and a fence surrounded the property with a large gate to allow entrance to the driveway.

My parents were great walkers into their nineties, so they thought that walking my older brother and I would be good for our health and also an energy reliever! Often they took my brother and me down to the gate, across the road, and into a forest area with little trails. There were always lots of fun things to see like squirrels, chipmunks, skunks, racoons, and birds. If we didn't cross the road, but instead walked for over a mile along the road, we came to the park and playground. It was so much fun to ride the merry-go-round, slide down the slides, and be pushed by my dad high up into the air on the swings.

One day I decided to take a walk by myself down the driveway. I crawled through the gate and headed down the roadway toward the park. I didn't know how far a mile or two was. I was just walking, walking, and thinking that the park might show up. My little legs were getting tired, and I had no dad to pick me up and carry me home.

> *One day I decided to take a walk by myself toward the park.*

Back home, my mom noticed that I was not making any noise and called me, but I was too far away to hear. After searching unsuccessfully for me, she became very anxious and then panicked.

Having once lost sight of my own son in a large, high-rise hotel in Hawaii, I can now imagine all the thoughts that were pouring through my mom's mind. Did someone steal her son? Had he fallen in a well? Had a wild animal attacked him?

She quickly searched upstairs, downstairs, in the basement, and out to the garage, but there was no sign of Freckles.

My older brother was in school and my father at work. My mom ran to the phone, cranked the ringer, and told the operator that she had lost her son and needed help to find him. Would the operator please call the police and our neighbors? Soon, people arrived and the searching began, to all the nearby houses and properties and into the woods, but there were still no signs of Freckles anywhere.

How far could a two-and-a-half-year-old boy walk from home? They began to expand their search. Could he have walked over a mile to the park? So off to the park the officer went, and to his surprise, there, curled up and sleeping on a park bench, was little Freckles.

The policeman quickly put me in his car and drove me to my mother. What a welcome relief for my mother and all our searching friends!

∽∾∽∾∽∾∽∾

There is a spiritual message here for us. I was lost but didn't know it. And that's what happens in our lives. We don't know Jesus, or forget about Jesus, and we're wandering around, lost. Yet there is a Savior who wants to find us and to wake us up from our sleeping, and who asks us to follow Him, to be safe in Him, and never to be lost again. As Jesus Himself said to us, "For the Son of Man is come to save that which was lost" (Matt. 18:11, KJV).

Sabbath Baths and Hot Rocks

Revelation Style—1947

I can remember being a five-year-old on Sunday mornings, walking down the street from our Fort Langley home past the public school to our Sunday school. Our family looked forward to learning about Jesus each week, and we really enjoyed studying our Bibles. One day a man knocked on our door and asked my parents if they would like to study the Bible right at home; particularly, the book of Revelation (this book, with all sorts of symbolism, can be very hard to understand). Wow, what a great opportunity!

> *One day a man knocked on our door and asked my parents if they would like to study the Bible right at home.*

Their interest piqued, they said yes. So once a week after supper, this Bible worker would come by and bring his big charts with weird looking and scary animals. I would sometimes have nightmares, seeing these wild animals, and somehow wake up with a wet bed.

As the Bible studies progressed, my parents learned more about health, diet, exercise, fresh air, and sunshine. My dad used to roll his own cigarettes and blow smoke rings for us boys (we thought that was really cool, although, fortunately, none of us boys took up smoking), but he soon gave up his tobacco habit. Alcohol was never in our home to begin with, thank God.

My parents soon learned the difference between the traditions of man and God's commandments as they are stated in His law, known as the Ten Commandments. They found that the fourth commandment said to remember the Sabbath day, the seventh day, and to keep it holy. So they started to go to church on Saturday as we began to keep the Sabbath day holy.

ఈ-ఈ-ఈ-ఈ-ఈ

A New School

There was a Seventh-day Adventist church school about seven miles from our home, and my parents thought LeRoy and I should go there. Thus, we withdrew from public school and rode our bikes each morning seven miles to the church school instead.

I was too short to reach the pedals, so my dad put blocks on the pedals, took the seat off, and wrapped a gunnysack around it. No problem now! Off to school we went each morning; rain, wind, sunshine, or snow for our seven mile ride.

On winter mornings we arrived at school partially frozen, and it would take us an hour to thaw out so that we could hold a pen and write. My brother and I got first prize for the best attendance and never being late ... even though we were the farthest from the school.

ఈ-ఈ-ఈ-ఈ-ఈ

Home Life

Sabbaths were always very special days for our family. Dad did not have to work, so it was good family time. We would usually have church friends come to our home for lunch after church, or we would go to our friend's house, where we boys would have a great time with the other children.

Fridays were also special days as we got ready for Sabbath. Mom prepared food, and we all had our chores, which included being sure that the wood box and coal boxes were full along with kindling wood.

> *Sabbaths were always very special days for our family.*

You see, our home had neither electricity nor running water. It did have a nice wood and coal stove with a large water jacket (a metal compartment attached to the side of the stove) for hot water. We also had a nice bathtub.

LeRoy and I would get our three gallon water buckets and hike across our property to our neighbor, Mr. John, who had said that we could pump water from his well anytime we wanted. A bucket with water was always beside the pump. This was priming water: you would pour some down the pump shaft and start pumping as fast as you could. Soon water would begin to flow out of the spout. If you went too slowly, only a small stream would come. But if you pumped fast, a large stream would fill up the bucket quickly. LeRoy and I would have contests to see who could fill their bucket faster.

It took many trips to fill our bathtub. Then Mom would bring hot water from the water jacket. With six in the family, the first one in the tub was the lucky one. After our baths, we would have family worship and then head off to bed. We had no heat in the house except for our kitchen stove and the fireplace, so during winter our bedrooms were like deep freezers.

Hot Rocks

In wintertime it was bedtime with hot rocks. We would place large rocks the size of dinner plates in the kitchen oven a few hours before bedtime. Just before bed we boys would make a trip to the outhouse, come back in and get our hot rocks (wrapped in a towel), then head off to bed. Those hot rocks helped keep us warm at night.

Mornings came quickly, and the day's routine would begin once again. My first chore was to empty the stove's ashes. It was fun because the hot ashes would make steam when I dumped them on the cold, wet ash pile. It would then harden, and I could make roads and tunnels. It was a fun place to play with my cars and trucks.

Next, it was off to the chicken coop. The hens always seemed happy to see me. It felt so warm and cozy when I slid my hand under the hens' bottoms to retrieve the eggs. Then I was off to the small barn to milk the goat. I did not like goat's milk, but my cat did. She would come by, open her mouth, and I would squirt a fair amount of milk straight into her mouth instead of into my bucket. Mom just thought we had a poor goat unable to produce much milk.

Life was simple then but always fun, because we were family. I look back very fondly on my loving parents who, though poor, provided what all the money in the world could never do: unconditional love; the same kind of love that God has for us.

> *Life was simple then but always fun, because we were family.*

The Christmas Beggar's Present

It was Christmas season at our house in Fort Langley, British Columbia. We went out and cut down a pine tree, then my dad made a wooden stand and set it up in the corner of our living room. It smelled so nice inside! We constructed paper ornaments and decorated the tree. My brother and I couldn't wait for Santa Claus to bring his presents.

On Christmas Eve, we hung stockings on our bunks. LeRoy slept on the bottom, I the top. We lay awake waiting for Santa, imagining his reindeer and sleigh stopping on our roof before the jolly man himself, with his big belly and red winter clothes, would slide down our chimney lugging a bag full of toys.

Even though for us kids it seemed as if Christmas would never come, morning finally did arrive, for sleep overcame us, and we woke to find our stockings full. Jumping out of bed and grabbing them, we ran to mom and dad's bed, climbed up, and showed them our stockings, which were jammed with apples, oranges, plums, socks, mittens, and small toys. They always seemed to be as surprised as we were by what was in them.

Then we ran out to the living room to see the Christmas tree and all the presents so beautifully wrapped. On Christmas Eve mom had put a glass of milk and some cookies on a plate and set it by the fireplace for Santa Claus. Now we looked at the fireplace, and because the milk and cookies were gone, we figured that Santa had come! Santa had such a big, round belly because, we thought, at every boy's and girl's house he would get milk and cookies.

We quickly got dressed and did our morning chores; emptying the stove's ashes, bringing in the kindling, wood, and coal, and feeding our French bulldog, Buster. Dad took newspaper and kindling and lit fires in the stove and the fireplace. Mom made breakfast, but we were not really interested in food; we just wanted to open our presents. We quickly ate, did the dishes, and had family worship.

Then, just as the time came to open the presents, there was a knock on the door. *Who could be at our door on Christmas morning?* we wondered. We wanted to open our presents! Mom went to the door, and there stood an elderly man in tattered clothes, holding an empty can in his bare hands.

> Then, just as the time came to open the presents, there was a knock on the door.

"Ma'am, can you spare some hot water?" he asked, looking feeble, cold, even desperate.

"Please," my mom said, once she was over the shock of meeting the sad figure, "please come in and get warmed up."

He shook his head and asked, "Just some warm water, please, Ma'am."

She then took the empty can which he held out to her and handed it to my father, who I'm sure was also surprised at the sad sight.

My dad quickly went to the water jacket on the side of our stove and poured hot water into the can until it was full.

"This will warm your hands," my dad said, handing it back to the man. My mom brought a cereal box full of food and cookies and gave it to him. He thanked them, turned, and walked away, vanishing into the frigid morning.

Here we were in a warm house, with warm beds and warm food, and there was this man, once a mother's little boy, out in the cold and needing to beg warm water to keep his hands from freezing. Something seemed so off-kilter to me, even as a kid young enough to still believe in Santa Claus.

We went back and opened our presents in our warm house with our loving parents and food and love and everything you could ever want, while out there somewhere this man was wandering in the cold.

෴෴෴෴

Christmas has never been quite the same for me since. With every Christmas I think of that beggar and Jesus's words, "Assuredly, I say to you, inasmuch as you did it to one of the least of these My brethren, you did it to Me" (Matt. 25:40).

To this day the image of the beggar asking for warm water has stayed with me vividly. One truth hit me hard from the experience: it is, indeed, more blessed to give than to receive. And that knowledge, which has stayed with me for all these decades, was the Christmas beggar's present to me ... the only present from that morning which I can still remember.

Buster's Broomstick Dilemma

Buster, our French bulldog, was my best, four-legged friend. Wherever I went Buster was with me to play and to tease me. He didn't have good looks: his nose appeared as if he had run into a cement wall and it got pushed flat. He snored and slobbered too, but I didn't care. I loved that little dog with his one-inch, stubby tail always wagging back and forth.

If I threw a stick, he would quickly retrieve it and bring it back to me, but as soon as I reached to take it out of his mouth, he would dodge me and run, only to come back for another trial. "Let's play a trick on Buster," I said to LeRoy one day, "and teach him to let go of the stick."

> "Let's play a trick on Buster," I said to LeRoy one day, "and teach him to let go of the stick."

We got one of mom's old broomsticks, and LeRoy held one end while I held the other down low for Buster to grab. He soon locked his teeth on the broom handle and would not let go. We dragged him over to our clotheslines, lifted him off the ground, and placed the broom handle on the two lines.

There was Buster, snuffling and snorting, swinging back and forth. But he wouldn't let go of the broom handle! He had amazing strength in his jaw muscles, and we stood and laughed at him until finally, after a few minutes, he began to get tired, opened his mouth, and dropped to the ground.

Every time after that, when we gave him a stick, he would get it, but as soon as we tried to lift him up, he would drop the stick. No more hanging on the clothesline for Buster! He learned his lesson, that's for sure.

And I think that we can learn a lesson, too, from this story. Sometimes, boys and girls, we get a stubborn streak, don't we? That is, we want to do what we want, no matter what. And, well, then our parents need to hang us up on a clothesline! How much better it is to listen right away. Let's not be like the Busters in the Bible: "But they refused to heed, shrugged their shoulders, and stopped their ears so they could not hear" (Zech. 7:11).

Scalloped Potatoes and Macaroni and Cheese

There were two foods that I just couldn't stand: one, scalloped potatoes, and two, macaroni and cheese (those little curly tubes just didn't seem right for boys to eat). And when Mom made scalloped potatoes, they always had black, crusty areas. Oh, how I hated scalloped potatoes, especially those crusty parts! My stomach would ache just looking at them.

> *Oh, how I hated scalloped potatoes, especially those crusty parts! My stomach would ache just looking at them.*

But my mom always said, "clean your plate. Lots of boys and girls in the world do not have food. If you don't eat all your food, there will be no more until tomorrow morning, and certainly no dessert."

What was I going to do? Well, when you had a good friend like Buster, there was no need to worry about having to eat either of those foods, actually. Buster was always by my feet and beside my chair during supper. I would slip a handful of scalloped potatoes in my little fist and drop my arm alongside the chair. And boy, those black, crusty scalloped potatoes would just disappear! I was happy but a little hungry; Buster was happy and not hungry. It didn't matter; be it scalloped potatoes or macaroni and cheese, Buster ate it for me.

I think my mother somehow discovered my trick. But even if she did, she never said a thing, knowing that if my dad found out ... it might just be a pants-down showdown for me!

I loved my mom; always caring, always smiling, always positive in life. I never heard her complain or criticize anyone. Mom's life was a living sermon.

No matter what we do, Jesus always sees. But like my mom, He always has compassion and a forgiving spirit. "For God so loved the world that He gave His only begotten Son, that whoever believes in Him should not perish but have everlasting life" (John 3:16). This does not mean that we can purposely do wrong. No, we should never do wrong. What it means, however, is that if we do wrong, Jesus still loves us.

Buster and the Car Ride

My dog Buster loved to go for car rides. If my dad rattled the car keys, Buster would jump out of his box behind the stove and run to the door. As soon as it was opened, he would run to the driver's door and wait for my dad to open it. As soon as Dad opened *that* door, Buster would jump up on the seat, then over the top of it into the backseat on the driver's side. He would stand on the seat with his front paws on the window ledge and look out, as if he knew where he was going. Buster had many funny characteristics that kept us boys laughing.

☙❧☙❧☙❧☙❧

Aren't you glad God provided pets for us to love; to play and laugh with? Just think about what fun we will have in heaven sliding down a giraffe's neck, petting a lion, hopping with a kangaroo, being tossed in the air by an elephant's trunk, or snuggling up to an ostrich. God is coming soon, and He will share His pets with us!

> Aren't you glad God provided pets for us to love; to play and laugh with?

We should always be kind to animals, and never mistreat or abuse them. Never! Says the Bible, "A righteous man regards the life of his animal," (Prov. 12:10).

Ocean Bark

Buster was born without an epiglottis; that is, the little flap of skin that covers the top of your windpipe (trachea) and keeps water and food out of your lungs. This meant swimming was very dangerous for him. Somehow, he knew this, so when we went to the ocean, a lake, or a river to play and swim, he would only walk in the water. He would never go deep enough to swim.

One afternoon when I was about eight years old, we went to the Salt Chuck (Ocean Water Beach) to watch the tugboats floating the huge trees (called "log booms") along the ocean to the logging mills to make lumber. There was a wooden pier that went out in the water about 150 feet, then turned and extended for another 100 feet. It was like the letter L.

Inside the bend of the pier, the ocean water was very sheltered and provided a safe parking place for boats. On this day though, no boats were parked there. Instead, the water was covered with bark from the log booms. It looked like a big brown carpet that you could walk on (but of course, if you were to step on it, you would go under).

Buster was playing up on the beach when I walked out to the very end of the pier then called him to come. Down the hill he ran and onto the dock. Then, suddenly, he ran off of it, thinking he could take a shortcut over the bark to get to me.

Splash! Quickly Buster began to dog paddle, but water was

> Buster ran onto the dock. Then, suddenly, he ran off of it, thinking he could take a shortcut over the bark.

getting into his lungs and he was about to drown. I instantly ran around the dock, reached over, and pulled him up onto the dock. He sputtered and shook for a couple minutes, but then he was all right. Dogs usually don't get fooled easily, but somehow Buster didn't realize that floating bark was not made to run on.

As boys and girls, we can get fooled sometimes, too. We might see something in an e-mail, or on an iPad or cell phone or TV, or even in a print magazine and think it's harmless. But it may lead us into trouble, and we can sink into sin really fast, just as Buster sank really fast on the floating bark.

The story of Buster makes me think of this verse: "Put on the full armor of God, so that you will be able to stand firm against the schemes of the devil" (Eph. 6:11, NASB 1995).

Yes, we want to stand on firm, unsinkable ground with our Lord.

Saved by the Baby Buggy

Mr. Sage had a large cattle ranch on the slopes of the Canadian Rockies. Once he invited us to visit his farm. He had three children the same age as LeRoy and me, and we were also looking forward to seeing the horses, cows, sheep, and goats.

His barn was bright red with a huge hayloft, and Mr. Sage said that by going up the steps, we could play in the hay. "But be careful," he had cautioned, "not to climb the wall ladder into the hayloft."

We kids started running around and playing hide-and-seek. It was my friend George's turn to count. "I will count to twenty," he said, "and you guys all go hide. When I reach twenty, I'll say, 'ready or not, here I come,' to find you."

Off we went, hearing the numbers, "One, two, three, four, five, six, seven, eight, nine, ten ...."

At the bottom of the hayloft ladder there was a large baby buggy. It had four big wheels and huge springs that made it a nice baby ride, because you could push the bar handles and rock the baby. The kids liked to put a baby sheep, goat, or dog in the buggy and push it around. But my attention was on the hayloft floor, which was some twenty feet high. I thought, *if I climbed the ladder to the hayloft, no one could find me.* Somehow I had forgotten what Mr. Sage had said about not using the ladder.

> *I thought,* if I climbed the ladder to the hayloft, no one could find me. Somehow I had forgotten what Mr. Sage had said

" ... eleven, twelve, thirteen, fourteen, fifteen, sixteen, seventeen, eighteen, nineteen, twenty. Ready or not, here I come!"

I had just reached the top of the ladder, which was nailed to the wall. I reached over the top, expecting to grab onto a board railing, but there was no board or edge to grab on, just the flat hayloft floor. My hand slipped and

I was free-falling. Now it was my turn to say, "Ready or not, here I come," and come I did ... down twenty feet onto the baby buggy.

There was a loud *crash*, and that was more than the baby buggy could support. *Snap! Snap! Snap!* The old buggy collapsed under the weight of my fall. And there I was, cuddled up in the buggy, with a broken foot hanging over the edge.

My friends helped extract me and carried me to the house, where my broken foot was treated and splinted. It was embarrassing to admit that I climbed the ladder, specifically after I had been told not to. Again I had to learn my lesson the hard way! And a painful way, too.

છે~જી છે~જી છે~જી છે~જી

Parents have the insight to protect us and guide us, but when we don't follow their advice, we have to pay a price, and sometimes it really hurts.

Jesus didn't disobey or sin, but He had to pay a painful price with His body on the cross ... because of our sins, not His. "He Himself bore our sins in His body on the tree, that we might die to sin and live to righteousness. By His wounds you have been healed" (1 Peter 2:24, ESV). Let's always be thankful for what Jesus has done for us, and for the hope of eternal life that we can have in Him. Meanwhile, obey your parents.

Fire in the Toy Box

It was a warm, summer evening in Fort Langley, BC. Our family was walking down the street to visit the Spensors, friends who owned the local, aptly-named Spensors' General Store. In the 1940s, a general store was exactly that: "general." It was something like a Walmart is today, only in miniature. You could buy almost anything: tools, toys, meat, beans, fish, eggs, potatoes, kitchen wares, rubber boats, shoes, hats, clothes, raincoats, shovels, clocks, kerosene, and more.

Fort Langley had the general store, post office, church, gas station, and public school ... and not a whole lot more. It also had a two-horse fire department which consisted of a firehouse, the fire water wagon, and a small barn for the horses. On the roof of the firehouse was a large fire bell, whose sound could be heard all through the town. (Fire hydrants were invented in 1801 by Frederick Graph, chief engineer of the Philadelphia, USA, waterworks department. In Canada, the first Macavity fire hydrant was made in 1903. We certainly did not have the luxury of a fire hydrant in the 1940s in Fort Langley.)

It was after 6:00 p.m. when we reached the Spensors', and the store was closed, so we climbed the back stairs to the second floor, where they lived. They had a son and daughter the same age as my brother LeRoy and me. Mr. Spensor welcomed us in and then told us kids to go play in the children's bedroom, where the toys were.

As we were playing, I began to scavenge around in the toy box and found some paper matches. These were just like the ones my dad used to light his cigarettes. Many times I had watched him rub a match on the rough part of the cover in order to light a cigarette. Imitating him, I rubbed the match head along the edge, and suddenly the match lit up. The fire scared me, and I threw the lighted match into the toy box, then went on playing.

> *I rubbed the match head along the edge, and suddenly the match lit up.*

Soon someone smelled smoke, and we looked into the toy box. The toys were on fire!

We yelled, "Fire! Fire!"

At first, our parents thought that we were just playing. Then, by the tone of our voices, they realized we meant it ... and they came running.

"Quick, call the fire department!" my dad yelled.

Mr. Spensor grabbed the wall phone and cranked it fast and hard.

"Hello, this is the operator," a voice said.

"Operator," Mr. Spensor said frantically, "call the fire department, quickly! The Spensors' General store is on fire!"

Soon, we heard the fire bell ringing, and men rushed to harness the two horses to the water wagon. In the meantime our parents were pouring buckets of water into the toy box. By the time the fire wagon got to the store, the fire was out. Thus, the fire wagon and horses returned to the fire house, ready for the next fire, whenever and however it came.

Fortunately, the general store did not burn down. Now, though, it was time for the parents to find out what had happened. How had this fire started in a toy box, of all places? Who lit the match? they demanded to know.

All eyes were on me. I had no choice but to confess.

"I didn't mean to light the match," I began, scared and ashamed. "It just all of a sudden lit up, and so I threw it in the toy box. I am so sorry, Mr. Spensor!"

My dad used this as an opportunity to make an important point. "When you play with fire," he said, "you're going to get burned."

Back at home, just to make sure I got the message, we had a little bedside warm-up (I should have calluses on my behind from all the spankings). How that leather strap burned as it sent a strong message to my brain, which was, "Don't play with fire!" I never made that mistake again.

☙❧☙❧☙❧☙❧

Yes, I learned a valuable lesson, even if it was the hard way: if you play with fire, you will get burned. Like Eve. Like Samson. Like Judas. Fire is a tool, not a toy.

Fifty Bee Stings

On our property in Fort Langley, we had a nice, wooden house that faced an open field on the road which led to the local store, church, and school. Across the street Mr. and Mrs. Jud owned a small farm.

Mr. Jud had an old, gentle horse, and he would lead it across the street to our house to give us boys a ride. No saddle; just good old, bareback rides. They were always fun.

Out back we had a barn where we stored hay for Mr. Jud. Behind the barn was the chicken coop, and then a forest of pine and cedar trees. A fence on the right side divided our property from another neighbor's property, the Jones's.

There was a ledge on the side of the fence, and each morning Mr. Jones would put a bottle of fresh milk on the ledge for us. If it froze, it would push the lid up and the cream would rise to the top. We always thought that was kind of cool.

Not far from Mr. Jones's fence, we had a three-story beehive. The bees produced wonderful honey, and the honeycomb was my favorite part. When I sucked the honey out of the honeycomb, I could then chew the wax like gum. The bees made enough honey for us and some to share with our neighbors.

Country living was wonderful. You never had to leave your doors locked. Everybody knew everybody and watched out for each other as well. It was like one, big family.

After school every day, it was time for us to do our chores: cutting kindling, getting firewood, and bringing the coal in the house. Then, after our chores were done, it was time to play; we always played outdoors.

No TV, cell phones, Game Boys, computers, or iPads. We ran free and used our imaginations to play in the yard and barn and to swing from treetop to treetop. The one area we were not to play by was the beehive. Otherwise, we could run back and forth to our neighbors' yards and play with their kids until we either got called for supper or it was bedtime.

One Sunday some friends from out of town came to visit. They had four children, and our family had four. Wow, eight children! We were going to have a great time.

My dad said, "You are all to stay away from the beehives. The bees are busy making honey and they do not need your help."

> *My dad said, "You are all to stay away from the beehives. The bees are busy making honey and they do not need your help."*
>
> *"Ok, dad, no problem," I said.*

"Ok, dad, no problem," I said to him, and off we went. It wasn't long before we found ourselves close to the hive, but we did not see any bees nearby.

One of the boys said, "I bet if Freckles threw a stone at the beehive, it would make the bees come out."

"I don't think so," I said, "because they must be busy making honey."

"Come on," he continued, "throw a stone and see what the bees do."

So I picked up a nice smooth stone and threw it as hard as I could, and *bang!*, it hit the beehive ... but no bees came out.

"See, I told you," I said. "They are busy making honey and aren't going to be bothered."

"Freckles," the boy continued, "here's a big stick. Throw it at the beehive and see what happens."

"Do you remember what my dad said about staying away from them?"

"Yeah, but he didn't know if the bees were sleeping or making honey."

So I took the big stick and threw it, and it smashed against the hive with a loud *crack!*

Still, no bees came out.

"What is wrong with those bees?" someone said.

So I slowly walked up to the beehive and gave it a big kick, knocking it over.

"Help! Help!" I cried. Bees were everywhere: in my pants, in my shirt, in my ears, all over my head. I ran to the house, crying. "Help! Help! Help!" I continued to yell, as the bees chased me all the way, stinging, stinging, stinging.

I ran into the house and jumped up on the table. My mom started taking my clothes off, while my dad swatted the bees away. They started putting some cold compresses on me. I began to swell up, looking like a balloon ready to pop.

Over fifty bee stings! Oh, how I hurt! I was afraid that my dad was going to give me a good licking, but he didn't have to, because the bees had done it for him. I promised my dad that I would always listen to his advice after that. And believe me, I meant it, too.

※※※※※※

The Bible says, "Honor your father and your mother, as the Lord your God has commanded you, that your days may be long, and that it may be well with you in the land which the Lord your God is giving you" (Deut. 5:16). Don't I know it!

Twenty Percent for Jesus, Eighty for Me!

Later in life I would be a student at Canadian Union College, and that life was good. Coming as I did from a poor family, finances were scarce, and I had to work my way through high school. I didn't mind. I had been taught good work ethics as a young lad; something that I have kept all through my life.

My first job came when I was nine years old. I was walking up the hill on my way home from somewhere when a gentleman standing in his driveway asked me if I would like a job cutting his grass. The payment: one dollar and fifty cents a cut.

"Why, sure!" I exclaimed, excited about making some money to buy a model.

I liked to build model airplanes and gliders. And so, once a week, I would come by Mr. Dubin's home, and he would have his push mower and a rake sitting in his driveway for me. After cutting the grass, I would rake up the cuttings and carry them to a compost heap in his backyard (Mr. Dubin would take the old grass when it got mushy and smelly and put it into his garden. He grew the loveliest vegetables with his mulched soil).

I must admit that it was hard pushing the lawnmower up his steep yard. At times I would be sweating. One day, to my surprise, Mrs. Dubin appeared with a cold glass of milk and a chocolate chip cookie.

Wow! I thought that I was in heaven. That cool milk felt so good in my mouth and throat, and that cookie stimulated my taste buds as it moved into my stomach ... a true, tasty delight.

When I would get home from cutting the grass, the first thing I had to do was take my dollar fifty and separate fifteen cents for Jesus as my tithe and fifteen cents as an offering to help with church expenses and missions. Seventy cents were put away in savings. With the fifty cents left over, I could buy my airplane parts.

I knew how to do this because, when I was very young, my dad sat me down and placed ten pennies out on the table in order to teach me about Malachi 3:8; about not robbing God of tithes and offering. He pulled one penny aside and said, "This represents the tithe; ten percent." Then he pulled another penny aside and said, "This is another ten percent for offering to support the church and its mission work.

> When I was very young, my dad sat me down and placed ten pennies out on the table in order to teach me about Malachi 3:8.

"The eight pennies left," he said, "are for you."

Jesus, he then explained, owned all the pennies but asks us for only two so that we can show Him our love. The difference sounded pretty good to me: 20 percent for Jesus and 80 percent for me.

That is what we call double tithing. Is that not a good deal?

❧❧❧❧❧

You know, boys and girls, many times I didn't have enough money for the things I wanted, but I have always had enough for what I needed. You cannot outgive Jesus, who gave His life for us on the cross.

The Bible says, "Bring ye all the tithes into the storehouse, that there may be meat in mine house, and prove me now herewith, saith the Lord of hosts, if I will not open you the windows of heaven, and pour you out a blessing, that there shall not be room enough to receive it," (Mal. 3:10, KJV). I have tested God on this ("prove me," He said), and He always keeps His promises.

The Disappearing Purse

It was a beautiful spring day, and my seven-mile ride home from church school seemed to go fast, as there were lots of things in nature to look at as I pedaled along. Halfway home there was a food processing plant, where the farmers brought their apples, pears, grapes, and other produce. I would pull into their driveway and ride my bike to the back of the building, where the farmers unloaded produce.

There was a very friendly gentleman worker there who was always smiling and seemed happy to see me. I felt that he understood kids and knew what they liked. He must have had a loving heart like Jesus. He would offer me an apple, a pear, or some fresh grapes to munch on as I rode home.

When I arrived my mother was always there to greet me and give me a hug and kiss. Buster greeted me too, with his little tail stub wagging like a wound-up spring. Then it was time to do my chores; filling the coal and wood box, cutting the kindling, and filling the water jacket on the stove with fresh water that I pumped from the well.

After chores it was playtime before supper. My neighbor friend Rex came over to play, and we began to think of fun things to do. I asked my mom if she had an old purse that we could play with, and she found one for me. She had kind of a funny look on her face but must have felt that two mischievous boys couldn't get into too much trouble with an old purse, so she didn't ask any questions.

Out the door I went and said, "Rex, I've got the purse. Let's go to the work shed and get some fishing line."

"Freckles," Rex asked, "what are we going to do with a purse and fishing line?"

> *"Freckles," Rex asked, "what are we going to do with a purse and fishing line?" "We are going fishing, so come with me," I responded.*

"We are going fishing, so come with me," I responded.

Out through the gate, down the driveway hill, and to the local highway we went. Alongside the highway were tall bushes that we could hide in.

"Ok, Rex," I said, "you need to tie the fishing line to the purse handle and set the purse on the highway, then come and hide in the bushes with me." This was going to be fun.

I heard a car coming. The driver saw the purse and hit the brakes, skidding to a stop. He backed up to where he thought the purse was, but in the meantime, we had reeled it in. The driver got out of his car and walked around to the back to pick up the purse, but there was none. He got down on his knees, looking under the car, but could not find a purse. He stood up, scratching his head, looking around and muttering.

We could hardly keep from laughing as he walked to his car and drove off. Once he was gone, we burst out laughing in the bushes. This was just too funny. We put the purse bait back on the road and then hid in the bushes again, waiting for our next victim.

Soon we heard another car coming, and the driver, seeing the purse, quickly came to a stop. Just like the last man, he backed up to where he thought the purse was, got out of the car, and walked around to the back ... but alas, no purse. Then he, too, got down on his knees and looked all around under the car: still no sign of it. He stood up, muttering to himself, got back in his car, and departed. Once more we burst out laughing in the bushes.

This was so much fun that we decided to try it one more time. Soon we heard yet another car coming. The lady driver saw the purse, quickly slowed down, and then stopped. Like the others, she got out and walked back to discover there was no purse. She stood still for a moment, looking all around, not seeing anything or anyone, then cautiously pulled up her skirt above her knees so she could kneel on the road and look under the car. She got back up and said, out loud so that we could hear, "I know I saw a purse on the highway. How could it just disappear? Wait till I tell my husband about this. He will think I've gone crazy." She drove off, and again we laughed and rolled in the bushes with tears running down our faces.

Fishing line and purse in hand, we walked back to my house to tell my mother what fun we had had with her purse. With a big smile on her face, my mother said, "you boys are lucky the police did not come by and fish *you* out of the bushes."

In Matthew 17:27 Jesus used a fish's mouth for His "purse." He wanted to have some fun with Peter and to teach him a lesson as well. He told Peter to go catch a fish and open the fish's mouth, where he would find a coin. Peter was then to pay their local taxes with this coin. Peter must have thought, *I have been fishing for many years and have never seen money in a fish's mouth, but I will trust Jesus.* Each of us should trust Jesus as well.

I went to sleep that night thanking Jesus for a loving mother, for His protection, and for letting us boys play some fun tricks.

A Bittersweet Lesson

The Okanagan Valley of British Columbia, with its warm summer days and snowy winters, was a great place for a boy to grow up. To this day I have many memories—great memories—of that time.

One Sabbath after church, a farmer's family invited mine to their farm for lunch. We were excited. They had children, so we knew that we could have fun playing together. Plus the farmer owned cows, sheep, and goats. He grew corn, wheat, and oats; and he had a large garden with an incredible cornucopia of vegetables: more vegetables than you can imagine. One of his largest garden plots was a huge watermelon field. It looked so inviting to see these big, green bumps growing (many were enormous).

As we finished our main course, the farmer noticed that I was looking like a boy ready for dessert. He was right.

"I have the very best dessert for you today," he said, getting me all excited, "but you'll have to follow me outside to get it."

Outside? Dessert? I thought. *Did he grow cookies on trees? Did ice cream sprout in his garden?*

"Follow me," he said, and out we went ... to the watermelon patch. Not exactly chocolate ice cream, was it?

Pointing to one watermelon, the farmer said, "This looks like a beautiful, ripe one," and he bent over and picked it up. Then to my surprise, he walked over to another, beautiful watermelon and dropped the one in his hand on top of it. The one that fell split open, and he said, "Here is your dessert. Just stick your little fingers right in this watermelon and pull out big chunks of juicy dessert."

We kids ate our fill of watermelon, with juice all over our sticky fingers and dripping down our faces and shirts. No, it wasn't German Chocolate Cake, but it was pretty good anyway.

The next day was to be the church picnic, and the farmer said that he was going to bring plenty more watermelons. There were also going to be contests and prizes.

Sure enough, that next, bright and sunny morning, we were at the church school and people were gathering for the festivities: balloons to pop, apples to pick up from a tub of water without using your hands, baseball games, volleyball games, and races of various kinds.

One of the most fun races was the gunnysack race. You would get in a gunnysack and, holding it up with your hands, jump to the finish line. Because I was a fast runner and jumper, I really thought that I would get first place.

The starter gun boomed loudly, and a line of us excited boys and girls began jumping as hard as we could. It wasn't so easy. Some were falling down or bumping into each other. I plunged on ahead in a dead heat with another boy, and by inches ... I won! I could hardly wait for my prize.

> I plunged on ahead in a dead heat with another boy, and by inches ... I won! I could hardly wait for my prize.

When the awards were announced, first place went to me, and I was so excited. What would I get?

A big, ripe orange. *You've gotta be kidding me,* I thought. *This is first prize?* Man, was I disappointed. And to make matters worse, the kid I just beat out by inches got the second place prize: an Oh Henry! Chocolate bar. Had I known that, I would have let him beat me! What kid would not rather have an Oh Henry! Than an orange?

An Oh Henry! Is a classic Canadian candy bar with nuts, caramel, and fudge coated in chocolate. It was my favorite chocolate bar by far, and very seldom did I get to munch on one. They were also fun to eat: you could gently nibble the chocolate and nuts, leaving the central sugar core, thus making the candy bar last longer. It was a delight! Yet that day at the picnic, all I had was an orange to peel and its slices to eat.

ॐ⋆ॐ⋆ॐ⋆ॐ⋆ॐ

It was, I would like to say, a bittersweet experience. Back then, in more ways than one, it was more bitter than sweet. Of course, looking back now, I think that the Lord was giving me a message that an orange is much healthier for you than is a candy bar. Fiber, vitamins, and minerals in contrast to sugar and fat, which are not good for you at all.

As a young boy, I wasn't buying that message. After all, the chocolate bar had nuts ... and aren't they good for you? That, at least, was how I tried to rationalize it back then. But today, especially as a physician and an octogenarian, I am so thankful for the all the beautiful fruit; so many different kinds that God provides, and that literally grow on the trees.

It is a powerful revelation (if we would but open our eyes) of God's love. He grows oranges and apples and bananas and on and on; not Oh Henry! Bars, which should send us a message. And part of that message is, "Oh, taste and see that the LORD is good; Blessed is the man who trusts in Him!" (Ps. 34:8).

The First Canadian Female Astronaut

It was springtime in the Okanagan Valley, and my mom and dad thought it would be nice to visit a couple of widowed ladies and cheer them up. Little did they know what kind of cheer two adventurous boys could come up with! I never meant to do mischievous things when I was a boy. They just seemed to happen to me (but not to my brothers).

We arrived at the ladies' home and went to their backyard garden to visit. They had nice, wooden sun chairs with large spaces between the sitting boards. The two ladies sat a few feet apart, facing my mom and dad. They were so happy to have visitors and to watch us boys scampering around.

Talking to old people was a little boring for us boys, and so we began to check out the backyard. We soon discovered a large garden hose that ran from the house right under the chairs into the garden. I checked the end of the hose, which sat under one of the ladies' chairs, and saw that no water was coming out. So I told LeRoy to watch, while I went to the house to turn the tap, because I couldn't tell which way was on.

I turned the tap all the way to the left and ran back over to LeRoy, who was holding the end of the hose, but when he pressed the handle, no water came out.

"LeRoy," I said, "hold on, and I will go back and turn the tap to the right."

So back to the house I went and turned the tap all the way to the right. I just knew this was going to work. What I didn't know was that the tap was really fully-on already and building up pressure in that old hose.

> *Suddenly one of the ladies let out an ear-piercing scream, as she was jettisoned into space.*

Suddenly one of the ladies let out an ear-piercing scream, as she was jettisoned into space. There was a geyser of water propelling her into the sky, making her the first Canadian female astronaut.

My dad quickly pulled the hose out from under her chair, ran to the house, and turned the tap off. My mother caught the new astronaut as she returned from lift-off and settled her back into her wet chair.

Meanwhile, my brother and I quickly lay down in the potato patch, watering the potatoes with our tears from laughing so hard, but not for long. My dad followed the hose and found his two, mischievous boys.

"Ok," he said, sternly, "which one of you boys turned the tap on?"

He should have known from the start that it was me.

"Daddy," I said, "I didn't know I was turning it on."

"You boys come and apologize to the ladies."

After the apologies, my dad told me to go into the house. I knew what was coming; I just wish I could have had some of that cold water from the hose on the backside of my pants as my dad warmed them up for me.

I felt that my mom and dad must have been laughing inside themselves, seeing the jettisoned, screaming lady. But you can be sure that they never let on to us boys. My dad was a firm Scotsman who definitely believed in the Biblical principle of, "spare the rod and spoil the child" (alert readers will note that this is an Americanism that blends the words of Prov. 13:24 and 23:13-14, but believe you me that my rear end got the message in its purest form).

Later, to help make amends, LeRoy and I had to take all our pennies from our piggy banks and help buy the ladies a new hose, since theirs was kind of old and ratty ... even though, as we knew, it still worked well enough to send one of them into space! But as I look back now, getting them a new hose was the least we could do.

Two Boys and a Bushel Basket of Tomatoes

When I was about nine years old, we lived in Victoria, British Columbia. My best friend Paul and I went to church school together. Some days after school, I would go to Paul's house to play, or Paul would come to mine.

One warm, summer day, my mom said that Paul could come after school to play at my house. We were both excited and adventurous. When Paul and I came in the kitchen, my mom gave us a snack, and we then went out on the porch.

Our two-story house had a long veranda (porch) that ran the length of the second level. Right in the middle of the veranda was a bushel basket full of ripe, red tomatoes that my dad had bought for my mother to preserve for winter. Mr. and Mrs. Smith's nice, white-painted house was a short distance across the fence. As we looked at those big, red, juicy tomatoes, our minds began to play tricks on us.

> As we looked at those big, red, juicy tomatoes, our minds began to play tricks on us.

"I bet you couldn't throw one of those tomatoes and hit Mr. Smith's house," I said to Paul.

"I bet *you* can't," he replied defiantly.

"I could," I said.

"Well, go ahead," he said. "Try it."

"Oh yes, I can," I answered again as I picked up a tomato and threw it as hard as I could toward Mr. Smith's house. *Splat!* A big, red splotch formed on the nice, bright, white side of the house. The juice, seeds, and tomato skins slowly ran down it. We laughed and laughed.

"Paul," I repeated, "I bet *you* can't throw one and hit Mr. Smith's house."

"I sure can," he said, picking up a tomato and throwing it as hard as he could. *Splat!*

Off we went, one after the other: *Splat! Splat! Splat! Splat!* Forty splats in all.

Before long the whole side of Mr. Smith's house was pink with tomato debris. The basket was almost empty and we were laughing so hard we had tears running down our faces.

Suddenly the kitchen door opened, and my dad stepped out. The laughter and smiles stopped, and fear gripped us.

"Look what you have done to Mr. Smith's house and our winter tomatoes!" he bellowed, angry. And I mean angry!

"Son, you go to your bedroom. Paul, you go in the kitchen and Mrs. Guild will call your mom to come and get you." By the tone in his voice, neither of us dared to do anything but obey, and fast.

My dad soon arrived at my bedroom. I was shaking like a maple leaf in a windstorm.

"Son, you know that you did wrong, and you're going to have to have a *reminder on your behinder* that will send a message to your brain, saying, 'I will never throw mom's tomatoes again.'"

My many adventures and mischief as a young boy cost me a lot of spankings, and did they ever hurt. One day I had gotten an idea: if I slipped padding inside my underwear, the spanks would not hurt so much. It worked, at least at first, but I wasn't crying the next time my dad was spanking me, and he knew something wasn't right. He soon discovered the padding, which not only got me another spanking but also meant that it was always bare-bottom for me from then on out.

That is why he said that day, "Son, take your pants and underwear down."

Yes, those tears of laughter had now became tears of sorrow, as my behind got sorer and sorer and pinker and pinker. Yet the whipping wasn't the worst part.

"Son," he said, after he was done, "you have to go over to Mr. Smith's house and apologize."

Man, I didn't want to do that. Maybe Mr. Smith would give me a licking, and my bottom would look like a ripe tomato again. In those days, neighbors could discipline you, just as your parents did. And it was an acceptable custom, so I was very afraid of what Mr. Smith might do. If I didn't go, though, my dad would have to spank me again, so I slowly pulled on my underwear and pants and made my way to the Smith house.

I timidly knocked on his door, and Mr. Smith opened and said, "Hi Freckles." Then his voice changed as he saw the tears on my on my face. "What's the matter, Freckles?" he said.

"Mr. Smith, I am so, so sorry ... but I threw a tomato at your house." That was not quite true. Paul and I had thrown a lot more than that, but I was so afraid that I twisted the truth.

"Freckles," he then said, "let's take a walk around the house and look."

As we rounded the corner, Mr. Smith's jaw dropped. His eyes opened wide as he saw the whole side of his house splattered all over with smashed tomatoes. His white house was no longer the White House, that's for sure.

Mr. Smith could hardly believe his eyes. He turned, looked down at me, and said, "*A tomato, Freckles?*"

I was about to burst into tears again.

"All right, Freckles," he said, calming down, knowing that the problem, as bad as it was, could be readily fixed. "Get the garden hose, and we are going to clean this mess up, because if Mrs. Smith sees this, then we are both going to be in big trouble."

We got to work, and though it took a while, we got all the smashed tomatoes off of his house. In fact, as the side of the house dried in the sun, you could not tell that we had ever made it dirty to begin with. It was nice and white again!

"Mr. Smith, I'm so sorry. Will you forgive me?" I said again, still a bit afraid though truly sorry. I really knew that what we had done was wrong.

"Of course, I will, Freckles," he said.

I instantly felt the forgiveness. It was like a weight lifted off my chest. It even made my sore, tomato-red bottom feel better.

ಶಾ‌ಶಾ‌ಶಾ‌ಶಾ‌ಶಾ

You know, boys and girls, Jesus gave His red blood on the cross so that all the stains from our sins could be washed away and made as white as snow; just as white as the side of Mr. Smith house after it had been completely cleansed. In a way, Mr. Smith was just like Jesus to me; he not only forgave me when I said I was sorry, but he helped me wash my stains away.

Do you love Jesus today? If you do, then ask Him to forgive you for all your mistakes, and He will; and then He will wash them away. When you say your prayers in the morning and before bedtime, thank Jesus for His forgiving love.

The Nickel Car Key

It was a typical day at Victoria's church school, but soon it turned out to be not-so-typical. The principal had a little, four-door Fiat. Between the neighbor's fenced yard and the school was a paved driveway leading up to a bicycle shed, where we parked our bicycles. The principal would park his car between the fence and the school.

That day for some reason my mischievous, little mind thought it would be fun for me to drive the principal's car. I was 10 years old but had been driving cars on our home property for two or three years by then. LeRoy had taught me many tricks, and one of them was how to start a car with a nickel.

When you turn on a car's key switch, it connects the wires and completes the electric circuit, so that when you turn the key further or press a starter button on the floor, the engine will start up. LeRoy showed me how, if you put a nickel under the dash between the two wires on the backside of the key switch, it would complete the circuit, so that when you pressed the starter button, the engine would start.

I said to some of my classmates, "Would you like to go for a drive in the principal's car one day?"

With excitement they all said, "Sure, but we don't have a key for his car."

> *I said to some of my classmates, "Would you like to go for a drive in the principal's car...?"*

"No problem," I said, kind of proudly, "I don't need a key. Let's go jump in his car and drive around the school property."

Our school was a two-story building with the gym on the ground floor. On the upper level, the classrooms looked over the playground area. Thus, the principal could watch outdoor activity from his classroom.

Seven of us kids piled into the little Fiat. I wiggled my nickel under the dash between the two key switch wires, pushed the clutch to the floor, put the gear shift into neutral, and pressed the starter button on the floor with my other foot. The engine fired up.

We were in business! I shifted into first gear. As I let the clutch out slowly, we were moving. With a car full of laughter and giggles, we drove around the school property, really having a good time. However, as we went by the classrooms, I looked up and saw the principal looking down on us.

Our fun and good time, I suddenly knew, was about to end, and I was going to be in big trouble. I drove around the school and parked the car just as the principal arrived.

He said, "You students go to your classroom seats, and Freckles, you go to my office."

Somehow, I frequently got in trouble at school. So the principal and my dad had convened a little conference months before this incident. They came to the decision that if I got a strapping at school, I would get one at home, too. I didn't mind the strapping at school, but the one at home with pants and underwear down really got my attention! This double punishment certainly made me think twice about some mischievous ideas, but somehow, this day, I hadn't been able to pass on driving the principal's car. Unfortunately, I let Satan take over my life, knowing there would be a price to pay.

The principal soon arrived and asked me for his keys.

"Mr. Ford," I said, "I did not take your car keys."

"Don't lie to me, or you will be in bigger trouble."

"I saw your car keys on your desk and did not touch them," I said, very nervously.

The principal went over to his desk, and sure enough, his car keys were right where he had left them.

"How did you start my car?" he wanted to know.

"With my nickel," I said.

The principal looked at me with astonishment and then said, "You know, you could have crashed my car and caused injury to the other students. I am going to have to give you a strapping and then let your father know what happened today. Hold out your hands."

Whack, whack, whack, whack, whack, whack, whack! It hurt really bad and brought tears to my eyes. How I wished that I had not driven his car. My classmates could hear the strapping and my crying, and there was sorrow among them that they had gone along with my antics.

I didn't want to ride my bike the seven miles home after school that day, knowing the second round of correction was soon to be applied to my tender side. My father scolded me and with few words said, "Pants and underwear down!" Then a very powerful message was sent from my tender side to my brain in order to remind me about what I had done. It was never a temptation again, believe me!

❧✥❧✥❧✥❧✥

You know, boys and girls, every day, Satan tempts us. Next time we want to do something, we should just stop and ask ourselves, "Will my actions please Satan or will they please Jesus?" If the answer we hear is that it will please Satan, don't do it. If the answer is that it will please Jesus, then do it.

I sure wish I had followed that advice before I stuck that nickel in the principal's car! It makes me think of the text, "My son, do not despise the chastening of the LORD, Nor detest His correction," (Prov. 3:11) ... even if the Lord uses my dad and the principal to administer it!

Buster And the Potato Salad

As I have mentioned, Sabbaths were always special in our house. On one Sabbath we were particularly excited. Mom had made a huge dish of potato salad and placed it on the countertop for lunch. We were having friends, the Tresslers, home for lunch that day. The family had two boys and twin girls, and at this point there were four boys in our family. Wow! Eight kids can have a lot of mischievous fun.

My brothers and I couldn't wait to dig into that potato salad when we got home! Out the door we all went for church except Buster, who had to stay in his box behind the stove. We didn't lock up our house. We never did, in fact (most of our doors didn't even have locks).

> Who would come in our house on Sabbath, eat our whole lunch, wash the dish, and then leave?

After church we arrived back home, followed by our friends. What a surprise when we entered the kitchen! The potato salad dish was empty; totally clean, in fact. We were stymied. Who would come in our house on Sabbath, eat our whole lunch, wash the dish, and then leave?

Suddenly, a loud snoring noise came from behind the stove. Buster was in a deep sleep, his stomach bulging as if full of baby bulldogs. But the hound wasn't carrying pups. Rather, he had a stomach full of potato salad.

My dad said gruffly, in a loud voice, "Buster!"

Buster jumped up. He knew that he had done wrong. He headed for the door, ready to run away; a trek made swifter by the little boost my dad gave his tail end with his shoe. Out the door he flew.

"You boys and girls go outside and play," my mother said, resignedly, "and when lunch is ready, I'll call you."

Out we went around to the back of the house and down a rocky cliff to the marsh meadow. It was always fun in the lush, green grass and bulrushes, where birds and wild rabbits scurried away as we came.

I saw something else moving in the grass below: a garter snake, about four feet long. I picked him up by his tail and he swung back and forth. Buster saw the snake and wanted to play with it, so I dropped it. Buster picked it up in his mouth, right in the middle of the snake, and began to shake his head back and forth. The snake's tail flew up and down on one side, and his head up and down on the other. We laughed so hard that tears were running down our cheeks.

Then, suddenly, Buster stopped shaking his head. His stomach was sending a message to his brain, saying, "There is too much potato salad in here." Buster put his head down, opened his mouth, dropped the snake (which slowly curled up), and went *urp, urp, urp*. Out came the potato salad in a pile, covering the snake completely.

We rolled in the grass, laughing. Buster, none too happy, kept his head down and slowly walked away. He was, I guess, a bit humiliated.

જર્જર્જર્જર્જ

But there's a lesson here. God has given us wonderful food to eat. It grows right out of the ground, literally! It is there for us to enjoy, and it is good for us, too. And so, when your mom makes a nice meal, remember not to overeat. There's no need to stuff yourself. It might give you a Buster stomach.

Your mom's good nutrition will help you grow strong. Always be sure, before you eat a meal, to bow your head, fold your hands, close your eyes, and say, "Thank you," to Jesus for the food. The food will help you grow physically, and in thanking Jesus you will also grow spiritually.

When I think of this story about Buster from so long ago, I also think of this verse in the Bible: "Therefore, whether you eat or drink, or whatever you do, do all to the glory of God" (1 Cor. 10:31). Amen.

The Lost Pocket Knife

It was a warm, summer day. I had just walked home from my public school, which was a few blocks down the road. My mother had a glass of milk and a cookie for me. Buster was happy to see me and wanted to play. First, it was time for me to do my chores, then I had time to play before supper.

It was always fun to go back in the woods, climb the trees, and make little whistles out of the branches. Buster was always by my side, sniffing around and looking for little creatures to chase. I found a nice, little willow stick that would make a lovely whistle. I reached in my left pocket for my Swiss Army knife—and it was gone!

> *I reached in my left pocket for my Swiss Army knife — and it was gone!*

How could I lose my best, little pocket friend, which was with me night and day? I always carried my knife in my left pocket, but it was empty. I searched in my right pocket, and in my back pockets, but did not find it.

This knife was so special. It was like a portable tool kit, because it had a corkscrew opener, scissors, two different knives, two screwdrivers, a pop can opener, and even a saw. I could do almost anything with my knife.

I ran into the house and told my mom that I had lost it. My mother sent me back out to look at all the different places where I played: out to the barn, where the cats slept, but no knife there; into the chicken coop, but the chickens just clucked at me as if to say, "what are you doing here? It's not time to collect the eggs." Next I searched the wood and coal pile, where I would build roads and tunnels for my cars ... but it was not there, either.

I was so sad. That night at supper, my father asked Jesus to help me find my pocket knife. Before jumping in bed, I checked all around, in every corner of the bedroom; but still nothing. I knelt down and said my prayers, also asking Jesus to help me find it.

It was hard to go to sleep thinking about my lost knife. Soon morning came, but there was no knife on my lampstand to put in my pocket like I always did when I got up. Sadly, I said my morning prayer, again asking Jesus to help me. Then it was time for morning chores.

Taking out the stove ashes was usually fun, when I dumped the hot ashes on the wet pile, and steam would rise up like miniature clouds, but it was not fun this morning. I then went to the hen house to collect the eggs from under the warm chickens' bottoms, but this morning they just didn't seem warm. I couldn't stop thinking about my knife.

It was time for morning worship, and my mom prayed to Jesus, asking Him once more to help me find my treasured possession. Breakfast was soon over, and I grabbed my lunch bag and was off to school. I asked my teacher and schoolmates to look for my knife, but there was no sign of it. After a sad day at school, I went back home again.

Buster was there to greet me and cheer me up with his playful ways. After supper, we had worship. My brother and I sat on the sofa with its large, soft cushions. My father opened with prayer, and once again he prayed that we would find my knife.

As a little boy I did a lot of wiggling while sitting on the soft sofa cushions. I slipped my hands behind my back and down into the large cracks between the sofa cushions. Then, suddenly, my fingers hit something hard. I pressed a little deeper and wrapped my fingers around a familiar shape.

Wow! I quickly pulled it out and held it up, then said, "Look, Mom and Dad: Jesus just answered our prayers. I found my pocket knife!"

I was so happy to have my precious, little knife back. We stopped our worship story and thanked Jesus for helping me find it.

※ ※ ※ ※ ※

There's something else to think about, too. Suppose I never found my knife? It could have happened. But if we think about it, we always have things to thank Jesus for. So even if our prayers aren't always answered as we want, we should still thank Jesus, for we all have things to be thankful for.

The Bicycle Siren and a Hamburger Face

Riding a bicycle seven miles to school every day could get boring, so I found something to make it a bit more interesting: a bicycle siren. It looked like a can with a dome and a shaft coming out the top. This shaft turned the fan and created a sound just like a police siren.

I mounted it on the front fork of my bicycle, with a chain running from the bottom of the device to the handle bars. When I pulled the chain, it tilted the shaft onto the bicycle tire, turning the fan on and sounding the siren.

My dad warned me that the front fork of the bicycle was not a very good place to put it. If the shaft turned into the spokes, he explained, it would stop the wheel from turning, and I would go flying over the handlebars. But I was having too much fun to move the siren to the back wheel.

As I was riding to school one morning, my aunt Ethel passed me in her car (she had no idea it was me). I pulled my siren chain. My aunt heard the loud sound and thought the police were after her. She pulled over, stopped, and looked around ... but saw no police. I rode right by her, laughing to myself. She resumed driving and again passed me, and again I pulled on my siren. Once more, she pulled over, looking for the police. This time, I rode up to her door and showed her my siren.

"Freckles," she said, "you are always pulling tricks on people. Now go on to school."

> *As I turned off the main paved road to go down a gravel road hill that led to our house, I pulled my siren chain but something went terribly wrong.*

Coming home from school another afternoon, as I turned off the main paved road to go down a gravel road hill that led to our house, I pulled my siren chain but something went terribly wrong. The shaft went into the spokes, just as my dad had warned would happen. The bicycle wheel went around once and got jammed between the forks.

I was airborne. I flew over the handlebars and landed on the right side of my face, my head, and my shoulder. Sliding down a gravel road on your face is not a good feeling. I was crying with pain. The right side of my face and ear oozed blood, my freckles were scraped off, my knuckles were bleeding, my shoulder was cut and bleeding, and my clothes were torn. What a mess!

I slowly pulled myself up as LeRoy came to help. He put my bike off in the bushes and helped me limp home. When I entered the house, my mom saw me and just about passed out. My face and ear looked like fresh hamburger. My mom laid me down and slowly began to clean up my wounds, pulling gravel out of my skin and trying not to tear my ear off.

My face and ear were so scarred up that I was embarrassed to let anyone see me. When we went to church, my parents let me go upstairs and hide in the balcony so that people would not stare at me. Time is a great healer, but I looked terrible for weeks and weeks.

In time I had new, pink skin, but no freckles on the right side of my face for years and years. Finally, the freckles returned.

❧∽❧∽❧∽❧∽

Why did I get in this bad situation? Because I didn't listen to my father's sound advice. My right ear is deformed compared to my left ear, so I carry the scar of not obeying. Every time I look in the mirror, I'm reminded that there is always a price to pay for disobedience, and I am so grateful that we have Jesus, who is ready to forgive and wash away our sins.

Jesus still has scars from being nailed to the cross. He will carry those scars for eternity. But my scars will be gone for eternity when I reach heaven.

How can you not love a Savior like Jesus? I think of the famous verse, "Though your sins be as scarlet, they shall be white as snow; though they be red like crimson, they shall be as wool" (Isaiah 1:18, KJV).

Winter Wilderness Adventures

It was mid-winter in Vancouver. My father had accepted a job as a safety officer and first aid attendant at Babine Lake logging camp in the north of the province. This was going to be an exciting adventure for us four boys. No school meant homeschool and lots of playtime. Our house was sold along with all our furniture and our few possessions. With suitcases and boxes packed, we boarded the coal-fired steam engine in Vancouver. My dad had reserved berths (beds on the train) for our three-day train ride.

The Avalanche that Stopped the Train

I sat by the window looking out at the people on the platform. I heard the steam engine building up speed, *puff, puff, puff*, and we slowly pulled away. It was soon night and time to bed down in our berths. The *clickety-clack, clickety-clack* of the train's wheels was soothing, and I soon fell asleep.

When I woke in the morning, I looked out the window, and to my surprise, the train was not moving. In fact, we were back at the Vancouver train station we had left the day before! What was wrong?

Soon, a conductor came through and told us that an avalanche of snow had come down the mountain and covered the tracks. Fortunately, our train was not struck and wiped off the tracks. The engineer had had to back up, and we now had to wait two days on the train while the snow was removed. It was fortunate that my dad had reserved berths; otherwise, we would have had a very uncomfortable time sleeping on the hard seats.

In two days the engineer got the okay, so we slowly pulled away from the train station, with the steam engine huffing and puffing large clouds of smoke.

It was beautiful to look out and see the snow-covered mountains, brown bears, and an occasional grizzly meandering alongside the tracks. We also saw a large bull moose with massive antlers and a calf under his dewlap feeding near the tracks. The noise of the train did not seem to bother them. On the rocky mountain ridges, goats and sheep jumped along the rocky crevices. How those animals could run on the side of mountains is a mystery.

As the train went around curves, we could see the steam engine sending up pillars of smoke, making large clouds in the cold, winter air. We could also see the huge, iron wheels rotating, and on sharp bends we saw the coal fire burning to generate the steam to drive the engine wheels.

Two days flew by quickly. We pulled into the Babine Lake train station, where it was ten degrees Fahrenheit, and snow was piled up to the roof of the station. The surrounding ground was covered with three feet of sparkling snow crystals. The manager from the logging camp had left a flatbed truck at the station for us and hidden the keys in the toolbox under the seat. We loaded our boxes and suitcases onto the truck and tied them down.

The Moose in the Wires

With mom and dad and us four boys, the truck cab was cozy and warm. My dad started the truck, and we headed to our new home in the logging territory. We were soon out of the little town and driving through large pine forests on the narrow snowy road. As we came through the forest, the trees were left behind, and we crossed a huge flatland. On the right side of the road were telephone poles with wires between them. My dad said, "Look, boys, there is a large animal off to our right and coming towards us."

What big animal was running towards our truck? It was a huge bull moose with massive antlers, and he left a large cloud of snow dust behind him as he ran through the deep drifts. My dad began to slow the truck, and the moose must have thought he could jump over us. As he took a huge leap in the cold air, his antlers caught in the telephone wires and he came down on the road in front of us.

He was not a happy moose with telephone wires caught in his antlers. We were scared ... and so was the moose! My dad knew if the animal charged our truck and broke the radiator, we would be stranded, and we then could freeze out in the frozen tundra with no means of communication. Being in such a remote area, we knew that no other cars or trucks might come on this road for days.

> *My dad knew if the animal charged our truck and broke the radiator, we would be stranded.*

That moose was swinging his head back and forth as he tried to get free from the wires. He was also lining himself up to charge us because, for some reason, he associated the wires with our truck. My dad shifted into reverse and started to back up as fast as he could. Just as the moose was about to strike the front of the truck, the wires slipped off his antlers. Now free, he threw his head high in the air, turned, and ran into the snowfield, disappearing in a cloud of snow dust. My dad stopped the truck and thanked God for protecting us.

※※※※※※※※※

Roughing It

When we arrived at the lumber camp, a slab wood cabin was ready for us. It was about 100 feet from a frozen, snow-covered lake. Inside was a large room with wooden beds against the back walls, a stove in the middle of the room, and a kitchen area near the front door with a sink but no running water. There was also no bathroom. Some of the walls had cracks, so that you could see outside and feel the cold air coming in. This was true air conditioning! We stuffed the cracks with paper. Outside was a stack of wood for the stove and a kerosene bottle for our lamps (there was no electricity, either).

> *Some of the walls had cracks, so that you could see outside and feel the cold air coming in. This was true air conditioning!*

Right away, LeRoy and I were assigned as water carriers. We went outside and got the axe by the door and two water buckets. The ice on the lake was two feet thick; it took a lot of chopping to make a hole. We filled our buckets. There were a lot of small moving critters in the water, but our mom would filter it with a cloth then boil it so it was safe to drink.

Later, after we were settled in, our dad helped us clear snow off the ice for a skating rink. And Mom was always sure to have our school time each day: reading, writing, and arithmetic. But when that was done, as well as our chores, we were on that rink. It was great!

There were also lots of wild animals around our cabin. Foxes, bobcats, bears, wolves, deer, elk, moose, squirrels, wolverines, and many birds. The wolves and bears would come to our front door looking for food. You could hear them sniffing around. If I opened the door, I could be lunch for a hungry pack of wolves or a bear ... so we always had to be careful.

We had a special outhouse: a two-holer out back of the cabin in the woods. I always dreaded bedtime, because LeRoy and I had to go outside to our air-conditioned outhouse before going to bed (the twins were too little to use the outhouse—lucky them!). It was very creepy walking to the outhouse in the dark with noises like owls hooting, wolves howling, and trees squeaking in the wind. We would think about all the eyes that might be watching us. When finished we would open the door, burst out, and run as fast we could to the cabin. It was always a relief to be back in the warm cabin, have worship, and climb into our beds.

༶ঔ৵ঔ৵ঔ৵ঔ৵ঔ৵

Hootie the Owl

One morning there was a knock on the door. A neighbor was there, and behind him was Nelly, his horse, and a large sleigh with sides on it. He asked our mom if LeRoy and I would like to come with him across the lake to a small island and get firewood. We were excited when mom said yes. We climbed into his sleigh and heard him say, "Giddy up!" Off we went onto the frozen lake.

Mr. Bob had cut and stacked firewood on the island. He pulled alongside the pile, and we helped him load the sleigh with it. Then we climbed up on top. Again, Mr. Bob picked up the reins and said, "Giddy up!" to Nelly. She started slowly pulling the heavy load of wood. Suddenly, without saying "Ho!", Mr. Bob pulled the reins back, and Nelly stopped. We were under a huge pine tree with a large branch right over our heads. We wondered why Mr. Bob had stopped the sleigh. Then he said quietly, "Don't make any noise, and look up."

> *We wondered why Mr. Bob had stopped the sleigh. Then he said quietly, "Don't make any noise, and look up."*

Right above Mr. Bob's head was a young owl in the tree. He reached out, caught the owl, and gave it to me. He said, "You can take it home and feed it, and it will be your new pet." It was so soft and fluffy and warm. I put him inside my coat.

When Mr. Bob dropped us off at our house, we thanked him for the fun day and ran into the house to show mom our new pet. We fed the owl bread and milk and a little table food. He sat on the rafter or the back of a chair in the house and watched us. We called him Hootie, and soon, as he grew, he could fly.

He would fly around the house, and when we took him outside he would fly away but always come back ... for a meal. Hootie would fly away for longer and longer periods of time, and we knew that soon he would be able to hunt and care for himself. It was sad to see Hootie go, but we knew that he belonged out in nature.

The Honking Tree

One time I discovered that some of the pine trees near our house had large, soft bumps on the bark. I broke one of the bark bubbles, and sticky sap flowed out. It was so sticky that you could not wash it off your fingers without gas or kerosene.

> I loved to tease LeRoy, so I called him over, showed him the bubbles, and told him they were tree horns.

This'll be fun, I thought and found some large bubbles. Teasing was part of my make-up, and I loved to tease LeRoy, so I called him over, showed him the bubbles, and told him they were tree horns.

"Trees don't have horns," he said.
"Yes, they do," I said, "because I pressed one and the tree honked."
So LeRoy took his thumb and pressed on the large bubble. No honk.
"See," he said, "I told you so."
"You need to press harder for the tree to honk."
So LeRoy pressed harder, and suddenly the bubble broke. Sticky sap flowed over his thumb, as I said, "Honk! Honk!"

He tried to wipe the sap off, but now he had it on his coat and pants. I laughed until I realized he was coming my way. I stopped and began to run as fast as I could. But LeRoy was a good brother and always forgave me for the many tricks I pulled on him.

A Trapper's Work

One of the men who lived at the logging camp was a trapper, and he invited me to spend a couple of days with him to learn how trappers make a living. He would sling a number of animal traps over his shoulder and carry a big bag of animal meat for bait. We walked through the woods and looked for animal tracks. He knew the footprints of the fox, wolverine, badger, rabbit, and many other animals.

> *One of the men who lived at the logging camp was a trapper, and he invited me to spend a couple of days with him to learn how trappers make a living.*

The man would drive a large stake into the ground, attach a trap to it, and then place some meat bait in the trap. He set four or five traps during the day, and then we would go home. The next morning we would follow the trap route and see what animals were caught. If they had not already died, he killed them quickly so they would not have to suffer any more. He then skinned the animals and took the furs back to his house to clean them up.

Finally, at the Hudson Bay Trading Post, he would trade his furs for food and living supplies. The Hudson Bay Trading Company would then sell the furs to companies that made fur coats, hats, gloves, earmuffs, and other fur products.

❧✦❧✦❧✦❧✦

The winters were brutally cold at the logging camp, and my dad came to realize that it really was not a good place for my mom and us boys. So come spring, we moved back to southern British Columbia. We could go to school again and be near civilization.

❧✦❧✦❧✦❧✦

Yes, it was hard and harsh there, and I can't say that I was sorry to leave, but I have good memories of those times and always thank God for protecting us all during our stay there.

Frozen Tongue

It was the middle of winter in Vernon, British Columbia. We were living up on the mountainside, and it provided us a beautiful view: glistening snowflakes in the sunshine; at night, the city lights twinkling like stars down below.

To play in the snow and make snowmen and snow angels was great sport. To make snow angels, you would lay on your back and stretch out your arms and legs, moving them back and forth. Then you would get up, leaving your angel imprint.

From our house to the bottom of the hill was over a mile, which meant a great sleigh ride down and a long walk back up. But we didn't mind: it was worth the thrill of a fast ride down the snowy mountain. We would create a whirlwind of snow dust behind us, and we would use our feet to help steer. Great, great memories.

One afternoon, LeRoy and I donned our winter pants, coats, boots, hats, and gloves, all in preparation for a fun ride down the long hill. I had my trusty pocket knife in my pocket and was ready to go. We were going to descend the mountain on our CCM sleighs. These sleds have bright red, metal runners and a metal crossbar for steering. When you lay down on the sleigh, your face is right above the crossbar.

> My dad had warned us more than once: "Boys," he said, "don't ever put your tongues on the metal steering crossbar.

My dad had warned us more than once: "Boys," he said, "don't ever put your tongues on the metal steering crossbar. It is freezing cold outside, and the metal will instantly weld to your warm, moist tongue."

"Yes, dad, we will keep our tongues inside our mouths," we responded, only half-listening.

We picked up our sleds and ran to get a fast start, flopping on our sleds ... and the race was on. Who would get down first, LeRoy or I? The cold air was streaming by our faces, making tears flow across our cheeks. Around the corners we went. First, I was ahead of LeRoy, and then he would pass me. Back and forth we went, having a great time!

I put my head down to lessen the wind and, I hoped, go faster. I was determined to win. Though my mouth was just above the middle crossbar, I wasn't going to put my tongue on it. I could see the bottom of the hill coming up fast as I edged by my brother, and we both came to a gentle stop.

Wow! That was so much fun, I thought, *and even better, I won (at least this time)!*

As I looked down at my metal steering crossbar, my mind began to play tricks on me. *What if I just touched a little, itsy-bitsy part of my tongue to the cold metal?* Though remembering what my dad had said, I still wondered about just an itsy-bitsy touch ... and zap, my tongue was welded to the crossbar!

Man, did it hurt! I couldn't move my head, and I couldn't talk, either (you can't talk if your tongue is welded to metal). How would I get free? I tried calling my brother LeRoy, but all I could utter was, "We-woy, We-woy!" I pointed to my tongue, then I reached in my pocket and pulled out my knife. I muttered the best I could, "We-woy, cut my tongue off. We-woy, cut my tongue off!"

LeRoy took my knife and, with a shaking hand, opened the large, sharp blade. He said, "I don't think I can cut your tongue off."

"We-woy, We-woy, cut it off!"

LeRoy got down on his belly so that he was face to face with me, slowly brought the knife up, and cut my tongue free of the frozen, metal bar. Blood began dripping from my tongue. Again, did it ever hurt! I pulled my tongue back, but it just kept bleeding and dripping bright red blotches in the snow.

How I wish I had listened to my dad. My tears were freezing on my face, and I would have to pick up my sleigh and walk a mile back up the hill, with blood dripping down my face and onto my clothes. But LeRoy was a great brother and protector. He offered to carry my sled up the hill for me.

I entered the kitchen, and my mother took one look at my bloody face, hands and clothes. She knew it was time to clean up a disobedient kid.

My dad was a strict disciplinarian. He knew that using the rod in love would not cause a child to die. But he looked at me and knew that "the rod" had already struck.

Sometimes, yes, we can immediately suffer from our wrong deeds. Believe me, I know. In fact, to this day I can still feel the knife cutting through my frozen tongue. Yes, it is better to obey!

Uncle Tom and a Banana Split

It was a warm, sunny, summer day, and my dad had promised us boys an ice cream treat (such treats were few and far between when I was a kid). As my dad was driving down one of Vancouver's city streets, we noticed a man sitting on the sidewalk with his back against a brick wall. As we drove by, my mother said to my dad, "Drive around the block and go past that man again, because he looked a little familiar to me."

> We noticed a man sitting on the sidewalk As we drove by, my mother said to my dad, "Drive around the block and go past that man again, because he looked a little familiar to me."

My dad drove around the block and stopped in front of the man. He looked up at us, and my mother exclaimed, "That is my brother, Tommy!" Sure enough, it was our uncle, Tom, basking in the warm, summer sun. My mom invited Uncle Tom to join us at the restaurant, where he could have a warm meal and an ice cream treat with us boys.

As a youth Uncle Tom had been a tall, handsome, fun-loving young man. He wanted to serve his country and joined the Canadian Navy. Unfortunately, he picked up smoking and alcohol addictions. As a veteran he lived on a government subsidy, which he used to pay for his addictions. Try as he might, he was not able to overcome them, and his physical and mental health got worse and worse. He lived in a little, lonely, one-room apartment; his life deteriorating fast due to his devastating lifestyle.

At the restaurant as I looked over the menu, I saw the picture of a banana split with big scoops of multi-colored ice cream, chocolate oozing over the ice cream, and whipped cream with a cherry on top. My eyes were as big as saucers. "Dad," I said, pointing to it, "that would be the perfect one for me."

We boys enjoyed our ice cream, as mom and dad talked to Uncle Tom. They offered him help, but he was too ashamed and embarrassed. Having declined, he then said that he needed to go back to his apartment.

Communication with Uncle Tom was lost for years. Then, one day, my mother got a call from the Vancouver Police Department. They told her that Uncle Tom had walked out on the Lion's Gate Bridge and jumped 200 feet to his death in the water below. How sad it was to see what was once a good life ruined by Satan's addictions.

༄-༄-༄-༄-༄-༄-༄-༄

There are many preachers who tell their parishioners that when a person commits suicide, this person will go to hell. I believe this type of preaching is very misleading, and I am so thankful that God is the final Judge and not any person; not even the preacher. I'm convinced, in fact, that a number of people who have committed suicide will find a home in Heaven at Christ's coming.

During my work as a county coroner, I have attended many autopsies of people, young and old, who committed suicide. The Bible records many such men, Samson being one. Many things, from drug use to broken relationships to the general stresses of life, can lead people to suicide. But it is never the answer.

I think of the brother of one teenager who lost his life in an accident. The man became so distraught that he went to his pastor, who assured him that his brother was in Heaven, walking the streets of gold, looking down on him and just waiting for him to come, too. But the stresses of life seemed overbearing to him and so he, the living brother, committed suicide, leaving a note to his parents not to mourn because he would now be in heaven with his brother. What a tragic misunderstanding of death and what it means to die.

If you have lost a loved one from suicide, please place your faith and trust in God. He is the final Judge and knows the hearts of people in ways that we never can. God does not make mistakes.

When we get to Heaven, and the books are opened, we will see that God was just and fair in His dealings with all people, and we will be able to spend eternity with Him and our saved loved ones. And that will be better than any ice cream we could ever enjoy here.

I take comfort in these precious words: "The Lord is close to the broken hearted and saves those who are crushed in spirit" (Ps. 34:18, NIV).

A Handful of Blood (and a Fainting Brother)

In one of our homes in Canada, you will recall, we had a wooden coal stove which had a water jacket on one side. We would fill it, then the wood- or coal-fueled fire heated it to provide hot water.

Each of us boys had chores. One of mine was to cut kindling wood and to start our stove and fireplace fires. Our dad would cut a large tree down, then together, using a large, cross-cut saw, we would cut it into pieces. This saw was about six feet long with a handle at each end. One person would stand on either side of the log, and we'd pull the saw back and forth, cutting the log in sections of eight to twelve inches long. Then we would take the log and set it upright and, with a metal wedge and hammer, put the wedge into the wood and hammer it. This would spit out smaller pieces of wood. Then I could take a smaller piece and split it into even smaller strips, called kindling, which were used to start the fires.

My dad had some butcher tools left from his butchering days. One was called a cleaver; it had a steel blade about four inches in depth and about ten inches long and a short, wood handle. The blade was razor sharp. I could take a piece of the small wood and hold it upright on the ground, then, with my right hand holding it in position, I could strike the wood with the cleaver in my left hand (since I was left-handed). Just like the wedge and hammer, this split off a fine piece of kindling.

> *My dad had some butcher tools left from his butchering days. One was called a cleaver; The blade was razor sharp.*

One day I was not as careful as I should've been, and the cleaver came down on the lower, fleshy part of my thumb, making a large cut like a "U". Blood flowed freely. I dropped the cleaver and put my hands together, but soon my palms were full of blood. It was time to go find mom, for sure!

Buster knew I had been injured and ran ahead, barking and scratching at the door of the house. Mom sensed something wrong and opened the door, and I walked in, dripping blood everywhere. LeRoy, my older brother, was in the kitchen and turned around. He looked at me, then my hands, then at the bright, red blood dripping on the floor. He turned as white as a Halloween ghost, became as stiff as a board, and fell over.

Now, I thought that was really funny and started to laugh. In fact, the sight took my mind off of my cut. But my poor mom had two patients to take care of now. She sat me down and put a pressured cloth on my cut, then cleaned me up. LeRoy was by now waking up from his faint, and he crawled into the living room where he recovered on the couch.

Today it would have been a trip to the ER and stitches, but back then we were several miles from a doctor or a hospital and had no vehicle, except the motorcycle that my dad had gone to work on.

Fortunately my mom was the most loving and gentle nurse. She never complained but always saw the positive things in life.

❧⚜❧⚜❧⚜❧⚜

My laceration healed, of course, but I still carry the scar today as a loving memory of my mother.

Jesus, too, has scars; scars on His hands and feet that He will have forever ... as a memorial of His love for us.

The Bakery Cat

While I was a student attending Canadian Union College, I got a job in the school bakery to make ends meet. Part of me was sad that I did not have time to play on the hockey team. Having to work a lot to pay for room and board and tuition, I could get a little envious of friends whose parents could afford to send them to school, and who as a result could play hockey.

On the other hand, I always believed (still do) in the value of hard work, and I was grateful to have a warmer job in the cold months. Alberta winters were often brutal, with strong winds and freezing temperatures that at times dipped to forty or more degrees below zero. So when I got up at 4:00 a.m. and went to the cafeteria to bake bread for the day, it was with a thankful heart. And the job came with some unexpected excitement of its own....

The bakery was on the lower level, and there was a back door entrance and a kitchen sink where I worked. When workers came in the back door, a stray cat would sneak in with them. I'm sure that he smelled the fresh bread. That cat was a nuisance and always brushed against my feet and ankles. I would open the door and shoo him out, but he would soon be back to pester me. *How to be rid of this critter?* I wondered.

One day I found about ten feet of really strong string. I tied a tin can to one end and the cat's hind leg to the other. I hoped that the noise from the tin can would scare him, and he would run away and not come back. However, I didn't take into account that the cat needed a stimulus to make him run away to begin with.

Under the kitchen sink and behind the bread pans, I found a small can of kerosene. I knew that I had found my answer. I took a small amount and applied it under the cat's tail. The smell would drive him away, I thought.

It worked! I opened the kitchen door, and instantly a jet-propelled, hissing cat with a tin can clanging behind him flew out the door. However, I did not anticipate what would happen next.

The pastor was also heading for the kitchen door. As he came around the corner of the cafeteria, my jet-propelled cat got tangled with him. The string wrapped around the pastor's legs. The cat was hissing and scratching, trying to climb up his legs, as the pastor began to dance in an attempt to free himself from this mad, hissing animal.

> *Instantly a jet-propelled, hissing cat with a tin can clanging behind him flew out the door. However, I did not anticipate what would happen next.*

The pastor began to quote Scripture (either in Hebrew or Greek, I think). I found this too funny to watch, so I quickly ran upstairs into the cafeteria, out the front door, and back to my dorm room, chuckling all the way.

He never figured out who tied the string and can to the cat with the stinky tail, and I certainly was not volunteering information! And despite the hilarious twist of the pastor getting literally tangled up in my scheme, it succeeded. The cat never came back to bug me as I was baking bread.

ঌ❦ঌ❦ঌ❦ঌ❦

The moral of the story? There is none! It's just funny, that's all; and who doesn't like a good, innocent laugh?

Squawking Chickens and Screaming Girls

While attending high school at Canadian Union College in Alberta, I was very busy with dormitory activities, classes, and my early-morning job making bread for the cafeteria. At times things were a little dull, so my mischievous mind would think of some exciting things to do in order to add a little zest to life. I said to my roommate one day, "Would you like to help me with a little fun?"

> *At times things were a little dull, so I said to my roommate one day, "Would you like to help me with a little fun?"*

"I would be happy to," he said. "All your mischievous ideas seemed to be good fun and full of laughs. What would you like me to do?"

I explained that if we were to go to the chicken coop one night and fill a gunny sack with chickens, then take them over to the girls' dorm and let them loose in the middle of the night, it would cause some interesting excitement.

"I'm all in with you," he responded. "When can we do it?"

"How about two o'clock in the morning, tonight?" I answered.

"Sure," he said eagerly. "Let's go for it."

Well, 10:00 p.m. came fast in the dorm, which was time for the dean to turn the lights out. The hall monitor came by to be sure that we were in the room and ready for bed. Then I set my alarm for 2:00 a.m.

When the alarm went off, I woke, thinking, *that was a short night's sleep.* I rolled out of bed and roused my roommate. We quickly dressed and snuck out into the hallway to be sure that nobody was around. Further up the hall was a fire escape ladder, which we climbed. Pushing the ceiling lid up, we crawled out onto the dorm roof and quietly closed the lid behind us.

The moon and stars were bright, and the colorful northern lights of green, purple, and pink were dancing across the sky. We tip-toed to the edge of the dorm roof, then down the outside fire escape we went. We quickly ran to the chicken coop and picked up a gunny sack, then entered the coop itself.

The hens were very quiet, probably sleepy, preparing to make eggs in the morning. We quickly stuffed about twelve to fifteen chickens into our sack, then out we went to the boiler room in the basement of the administration building.

There were heating tunnels leading from the boiler room to the boys' dorm and girls' dorm. The tunnel was sealed off at the boys' dorm entrance (this was the administration's way of saying, "no boys are going to sneak through!"). But from the administration building, we could get in, bend over to a near-squatting position, and, with our flashlights on, make our way through a very long heating tunnel to the girls' dorm. There was a door that let us into their furnace room, then a second, locked door that opened into the basement.

Before she went to bed that evening, I had asked one of my trusted girl friends to unlock the furnace room, never telling her why (though she later learned). Thus, we were able to very quietly open the furnace room door, close it, and sneak up the stairway to the top floor.

We quickly opened our gunnysack and dumped the chickens onto the floor. The floors were covered with tile which made them very slippery, so the chickens couldn't stand upright. They were scared and began to squawk loudly, making some deposits on the floor (they weren't all eggs, either).

With lightning speed my roommate and I headed with an empty sack back downstairs to the furnace room. We could hear the girls screaming when they opened their doors and saw chickens squawking and trying to fly and stand up on the tile floor. The girls had no idea why they were being invaded by these boisterous birds, and they were as scared as the chickens themselves!

All the commotion and flying feathers set off the dorm alarms, bringing faculty to rescue the girls and the chickens. Meanwhile, locking the door behind us, we headed into the furnace room, into the tunnel back to the administration building boiler room, and finally out the door. At the boys' dorm, we went up the fire escape, across the roof to the fire lid, popped it open, and then climbed down the indoor, hallway fire escape ladder. Quickly and quietly we ran down the hallway into our room, undressed, and jumped into bed ... undetected the whole time!

The next day the campus was abuzz with the girls telling everyone about the midnight chicken visitors that had scared them to death. The girls' dean could not figure out how someone could enter the dorm in the middle of the night with all its doors locked. Our girl friend kept the secret, and no one ever figured out who the mischievous culprits were.

We felt a little bad for the dean, the faculty, and the girls, for they all had to round up the chickens and clean the hallways. But not too badly, I guess, because we were still laughing to ourselves about the chicken episode that next day.

ఒఙఒఙఒఙఒఙ

The Bible says that confessions are good for the soul. And so, after more than sixty years, I am now confessing for my roommate and myself. This is a funny story, yes. But just because it's funny doesn't make it right, does it?

Seven Rivers and a Drowned Volkswagen

It was summer in Alberta ... and Canadian summers can get hot. My friend Brian suggested that we load the back seat of his Volkswagen Beetle with our tent, sleeping bags, flashlights, kerosene lamp, and other camping utensils, along with a six pack of Orange Crush pop, hotdogs, and buns, then go camping in the Canadian Rockies, where there are lots of mountains, rivers and cool, cool air. It sounded like a plan.

༺༻༺༻༺༻༺༻

Off to God's Zoo

This was going to be fun. We were, indeed, "happy campers," going to enjoy the wilds of nature. This was God's zoo, where bear, moose, wolves, deer, mountain lions, buffalo, lynx, elk, fox, snakes, birds, and many other wild creatures made their homes. We didn't need water, as there would be lots of cold, fresh mountain water from the streams.

> We were, indeed, "happy campers," going to enjoy the wilds of nature. This was God's zoo.

We went to the gas station, lifted the hood of the VW, and filled the gas tank (back then Beetles had the gas and luggage in the front and the engine in the back). Then we left the city of Edmonton and soon found a little, country road off the paved highway. We began our journey into the Rockies.

Soon our road was just two bumpy ruts. We happily bounced along, going deeper and deeper into the forest. Coming out into a large, open area, we could see herds of buffalo and, in the distance, a ranger's cabin (rangers are like the policemen of the forest and mountains and are there to protect the wildlife, the campers, and to watch out for fires).

We drove to the cabin, and the ranger came out to greet us and to find out where we planned to go. If we did not show back up at his cabin in a certain number of days, he would come looking for us.

The Ranger's Warning

"Now, boys," he said like a stern father, "I have to give you some advice. When you look up in the mountains and see the snow, know that it is many feet deep and can turn into an avalanche. Also, as the sun shines on the snowcapped mountains, the snow melts, and the water runs down and can cause little streams to become raging rivers.

"It is morning now, so most of the rivers are small streams from yesterday's runoff. But as the sun melts the snow today, these little streams that you can drive through now will become too big to pass though later. By late afternoon when you plan to arrive at your destination, you will have to be very careful. The water will be so high and flowing so rapidly that you might not be able to drive through it.

> By late afternoon. The water will be so high and flowing so rapidly that you might not be able to drive through it. I want you boys to have fun, but please be very careful.

"You will have seven rivers to cross. I want you boys to have fun, but please be very careful. I will plan on seeing you in a couple days."

Whew! That was quite the sermonette, but we thanked him and off we went. Our first stream was, as he said, just a trickle, and we drove right through it. Looking to our right, we spotted a big, brown bear picking berries off a bush. He didn't pay any attention to us and kept on stuffing his mouth.

The First Six Rivers

Arriving at the second stream, we saw that it was larger than the first one but still no problem, so we went splashing and plowing right through it. It was fun! We were enjoying the scenery when, suddenly, a large bull moose walked out of the trees onto the roadway, his dewlap swinging back and forth. He didn't seem concerned about us. I blew the horn, and the moose, thinking (I suppose) that it was some weird noise, ambled off the road.

It was noon now, and the sun was at its peak. The third stream was a small river, and we went through, but with a bigger splash than we had on the previous two. It was then time to stop for lunch and build a fire to roast our hotdogs and down our orange sodas.

Enjoying the countryside, we paid no attention to how far we were from the ranger's cabin, and soon the fourth river, a little bigger than the three before, showed up. Again we went splashing through. No problem.

The fifth stream was a full-fledged river. Though getting a little concerned, we crossed it easily. The VW seemed to float across the water. The sun was starting to slowly go down. About 4:00 in the afternoon, we spotted two bald eagles surveying the mountain sides, gliding so peacefully. They were stunningly beautiful.

The streams were now all rivers. The sixth river was flowing rapidly, and we had to pick a spot that looked safe to cross. With a big, loud *splash*, we entered the river and popped up on the far bank. That was, I had to admit, a little scary.

The Seventh River

We still had one last river to cross before getting to our campsite for the night. What were we going to face? The sun had done its job melting the mountain snows, and as we approached the seventh river, we knew that we might be in big trouble. It was near 5:00 p.m. now and getting dusky. We didn't feel safe camping in the open mountainside, with all the wild animals roaming freely. We preferred the protection of a campsite, so we had to cross the last river.

> We approached the seventh river, which was raging and near the top of its banks.

Somehow forgetting the ranger's advice, we approached the seventh river, which was raging and near the top of its banks. We stopped, looking for the best place to cross. One sandy bottom area appeared inviting, but the water was very deep—too deep for our VW. It was flowing rapidly, too. In an alternative area, the water was shallower with a very rocky bottom.

The river was running faster and faster. We thought where the water was shallower was the best place, so we jumped back in the car, reversed as far back as we could, then got it up to a good speed. Into the river we went!

Stuck in the Middle

We made a huge *splash*, but this time, instead of floating across the water, the VW stopped dead in the middle of the river and nestled down between the rocks at its bottom. We had not anticipated the rocks separating beneath us.

The raging water was trying to push the car downstream, so we opened the car doors to let the water run through and prevent the car from being pushed downstream and rolling over. We were in big trouble now: I mean, the engine was underwater!

Cell phones were not invented yet, and we had no means of communication. We grabbed our flashlights and got the most important things: two cans of orange soda and the two left-over hot dogs and buns. We struggled through the icy, cold water to the riverbank. Not knowing how far ahead our planned campsite was, we decided to walk back to the ranger's cabin ... but did not realize how far we had traveled during the day.

ಹಿ-ಳಿ ಹಿ-ಳಿ ಹಿ-ಳಿ ಹಿ-ಳಿ

A Long Trek

It was now 6:00 p.m. and dark. As we walked with wet feet in soggy sneakers, we talked about the fun things of camping and how we wished that we had taken the advice of the ranger. We walked and walked. Midnight came with no sight of the ranger's cabin. It was very eerie at night to hear the wolves howling, owls hooting, and wind making scary noises in the trees.

Very tired, we paused to eat our cold hot dogs and drink our pop. We saved the cans to catch river water. Then more walking, walking, walking, but slower and slower. Brian did not exercise much, and he was having a difficult time. Fortunately, I exercised regularly, and although I was tired, I was okay.

It was now 3:00 a.m., and still no ranger's cabin. We kept on going, and soon it was getting light. By 6:00 a.m., off in the distant valley, we could see a small stream of smoke in the air. Hallelujah!

As we approached the cabin, the door opened, and the ranger greeted us. He somehow knew what had happened and said, "Come in and get dry."

"My wife," he said, "will have a hot breakfast for you boys." He told us that the seventh river was twenty-six miles away. That was a long night's walk! "After breakfast," he said, "I will take you in my four-wheel drive Jeep, and we will go to the river and pull your car out."

Our Wet Beetle

When we got there later that morning, the water was a stream. The VW was nestled down in the rocks, just as we had left it, with the doors open. The ranger took his winching cable, hooked it to the Volkswagen, and pulled it out of the river. We thought the engine would never run again, but when I turned the key on and pressed the starter, the engine sputtered and sputtered, then ran smoothly.

After all this our camping trip was over. We had had enough excitement and were totally fatigued. We decided we should head back home. We turned the Volkswagen around and followed the ranger back to his cabin, where we thanked him and his wife for their graciousness and then apologized for not following his advice. This man and his wife truly had Christian hearts.

The lesson that I learned from this? God has given us good commands in the Ten Commandments. And when we follow them, we won't so easily get stuck in the raging rivers of life. If we do get stuck, however ... He is always ready to come and pull us out.

Hospital Adventures and a Ouija Board

When I was a very young teenager, my father obtained a job for me in the local Catholic hospital in Victoria, Canada, as an orderly (a male nursing assistant). Some of my job responsibilities were to help with bathing, dressing, and transferring patients from bed to chair. I also prepared dead bodies and moved them to the morgue.

> *I slid my key into the old lock and, with squeaky metal noises, opened the door and went into the dark morgue.*

I didn't really like wheeling a dead body on a stretcher by myself down old, squeaky elevators to the basement of the hospital, where the morgue was located. It was very eerie. But it was simply part of my job.

One night at about 3:00 a.m., I had to prepare a deceased man, load him on a stretcher, and head for the morgue. Arriving at the locked door, I slid my key into the old lock and, with squeaky metal noises, opened the door and went into the dark morgue. I made my way to the center of the room so I could pull the string cord and turn on the light.

On this occasion there were a lot of bodies on stretchers. As I bumped one, an "urrr" sound emerged as air came out of the patient's mouth. It scared me to death!

I never got to the light string. Instead, I grabbed my stretcher, shoved it into the room, ran out of the morgue, slammed the door, and headed back upstairs.

A more interesting task was to ready patients for surgery. Back in the 1950s and 1960s, bodies had to be shaved extensively beforehand. The majority of the surgeries were abdominal and required shaving the men from mid-chest to the knees, including the pelvis area.

A number of the patients at the hospital were Ukrainian and did not understand English. One morning, I had a gentleman patient who seemed to understand when I asked and motioned that he needed to be shaved before his abdominal surgery. I had my basin of warm water, soap shaving cream, and towels. I very carefully shaved him from mid-chest all the way to his knees, leaving no hair. He seemed to enjoy the procedure, and I was quite proud of the nice job I did.

Just as I finished, a doctor walked in and asked me why I had shaved his patient. I told him that this was the order I had gotten from the nurse, "because you are going to remove his appendix."

The doctor had a smile on his face and said, "There has been a mistake. The one going for surgery is the fellow in the next bed, not this man."

I was really scared: I had shaved the wrong patient! I apologized to the man and his doctor interpreted for me. He and the doctor had a good laugh. I had to move to the next bed and start over again.

After finishing my morning shaving jobs, another patient called for some fresh water. When I brought the water to his bedside table, I noticed that he had a small board with the letters of the alphabet on it. Engraved on the top of the board was the word, "Ouija."

I had heard about Ouija boards and had been told that they were a means of communicating with the devil, but I thought the whole thing was a bunch of baloney. I asked the patient what it was and he said, "You ask me a question, and the spirit world gives me the answer."

> I had heard about Ouija boards and had been told that they were a means of communicating with the devil, but I thought the whole thing was a bunch of baloney.

"Really?" I said, not believing him.

"Ask me something," he said, "and I will ask my Ouija board to answer for you."

"Okay," I said, knowing inside that the board would never be able to answer, "what is my middle name?"

My mother's name was Phyllis, and I was named after her; Phil. It was a name that I didn't use, so few knew it.

He picked up the board and pointed to *PHIL*!

I was astounded ... and scared. I could not believe what I was seeing! I knew right then and there that I never wanted to have anything to do with Ouija boards, fortune tellers, psychics, or any other means of communicating with the demonic spirit world.

≈≈≈≈≈

I learned a valuable lesson that day: the devil is alive and well and he is going about this earth as a roaring lion to devour whoever he can (1 Peter 5:8). There are stories in the Bible about kings who sought communication through the spirit world of witches and false prophets. The outcomes were never good.

Keep your eyes focused each day on good things and the cross of Jesus, and the devil will not be able to lead you astray. And remember, too, that though the devil is alive, Jesus has defeated him at the cross, so we can find power and safety in Jesus. As the Bible says, "Therefore submit to God. Resist the devil and he will flee from you" (James 4:7).

A Doctor's Gift and a Broken Hand

It was Christmas break at Canadian Union College, and everyone was excited to be going home for a few days. That included my brother LeRoy, who had already graduated and was working in the school's printing press. I also had classmates from Vancouver and Victoria whom we were dropping off and later picking back up.

LeRoy had bought a 1938 Chevrolet. It was a four-door car, and all the doors opened from the middle of the car outward. The six of us, plus LeRoy, started loading our suitcases in the trunk. The trunk was too small to hold them all, so we stacked them up on the roof. Four of us sat in the backseat, three in the front, and off we went.

The heavy snow had been plowed off the highway, and we were able to climb through the mountain passes without having to put chains on the tires. We arrived without incident.

It was good to be home and to see my mom, dad, and my little twin brothers. Vacation went all too fast, and we once more loaded the car, picked up our classmates, and headed back to CUC.

We had gone through the highest mountain passes and were coming down onto the flatlands of Alberta. The roads seemed clear, when suddenly the car hit a patch of black ice. The car spun around and began to roll over into a ditch. Fortunately, the suitcases on the top of the car prevented the car from rolling totally over.

There we were with the car partially on its side and roof. Outside, antifreeze and oil were leaking from the engine. Inside, we were all bunched up together against the doors. I heard LeRoy say, "Is anyone hurt?"

One girl said, "My hand feels very, very painful." Otherwise, we were all okay.

Two cars came to our rescue. Two men climbed up on the side of our car, opened the doors, and helped each of us climb out. Soon other cars arrived, and all the men were able to push the car back upright. One of the men had antifreeze and extra oil and filled the radiator and engine oil for us. He would not let us pay. We were thankful to God for sending Good Samaritans and thanked the men for their kindness.

Joan's hand was swollen; I knew she had broken it. So we drove into the little town and took her to a doctor's office. The doctor asked us what we were doing way out in the country and where we were going. We told him that we were coming back from Christmas vacation to continue our high school education. He examined Joan's hand and x-rayed it, confirming a fracture. He put a temporary cast on to support it and to relieve her pain.

> I never dreamed of being a doctor but thought to myself, If I ever become a doctor, I will not charge someone in need.

I asked how much we owed him. Between the seven of us, we barely had enough money for gas to get us back to school, but the doctor did not know that. Even so he said, "You don't owe me anything. I'm glad no one was seriously hurt. Now have a safe trip to school."

Wow! I couldn't believe it. A no-charge doctor call. I never dreamed of being a doctor but thought to myself, *If I ever become a doctor, I will not charge someone in need.*

ಎ೯ಎ೯ಎ೯ಎ೯ಎ೯

Over all these years now, I have not charged many patients in need and have forgiven many of their debts, too; all because a country doctor taught me what real medicine is: helping others in need.

When you help someone in need, you are getting the best paycheck that one can ever get and surely reflecting the character of Jesus, who said, "For even the Son of Man did not come to be served, but to serve" (Mark 10:45).

Frozen Legs: The Mountain Motorcycle Ride

It was fall and time to return to Canadian Union College high school in Alberta. Living in Victoria on Vancouver Island presented a problem for a motorcyclist, because motorcycles are not designed to carry you across oceans. To get to Vancouver on the mainland required a long boat ride on the Queen Victoria. My brother LeRoy and I purchased tickets and rode his little 125cc BSA motorbike onto the ship for a night cruise.

Once off the ship in Vancouver, we headed south to the American border and passed through U.S. customs. The mountain passes in the United States were lower than the ones in Canada, which made it easier for us to cross over into Alberta. However, it was a strain, at best, for this bike to carry the two of us, especially through mountains. As the roads got higher, our bike went slower and slower, until I had to get off and walk to get to the top of the mountain ridge.

We had one last ridge to cross when the engine decided it did not want to carry us anymore. The valves burned out. We were fortunate to find a garage with an experienced mechanic who knew how to fix motorcycles. He repaired the engine, and we headed for the last pass.

It was getting very cold, and the rain became freezing rain and snow. Cold rain and snow do not mix well with motorcycling. We put newspapers in our pants but we were getting chilled through to our bones. We prayed, "Please, God! If

> *It was getting very cold, and the rain became freezing rain and snow. We prayed, "Please, God! If we could only get to the bottom of the slippery icy mountain road and find shelter for the night, before we freeze to death.*

we could only get to the bottom of the slippery icy mountain road and find shelter for the night, before we freeze to death. Amen."

We slowly made our way down the switchback mountain highway to some level ground, and we could see an inn's light in the distance. What good news! An answer to prayer!

We drove right up to the front door. Immediately, a gentleman opened the door and said, "You boys must be frozen. Come on in!"

These were the most welcome words that I had ever heard! However, we were kind of frozen in a sitting position and fell off the motorcycle. We struggled to our feet, and the gentleman helped us into the warm inn.

"I have a nice, warm room upstairs for you boys," he said, "and I will bring you some hot chocolate."

That sounded so good. We were so stiff and so cold we could only mumble when we tried to talk. We could walk up the stairs but only by holding onto the handrails and pulling ourselves up. It seemed like hours before we got warm enough to sleep.

Next thing we knew, it was morning. The innkeeper had a hot breakfast for us, and we filled our empty bellies and had happy tummies. The freezing rain and snow had stopped. It was still very cold, but we were happy get back on our motorcycle and head off to school. We soon approached the customs border again and passed into Canada and onto our destination, Canadian Union College. We travelled with thankful hearts for God having kept us safe.

༺✦༻✦༺✦༻✦

It's easy to forget how often God does protect us. That's why it's important to always have a thankful heart.

The Missing Motorcycle

Just prior to graduating from Canadian Union College High School, my classmate and I went to a motorcycle shop where we each purchased a brand-new Triumph 1000cc motorcycle. A 1000cc was the biggest Triumph engine that you could buy. Those light blue bikes were beautiful.

It was a thrill to have all that power between your legs and race down the highway up to a top speed of 115 miles per hour. Speeding on a motorcycle was not a good thing, but we were young and foolish. We also found that if we took the mufflers off of the motorcycles, they were much more noisy, and this modification could create some real excitement.

At night we could go out on the highway and, with our lights on, ride side-by-side to simulate a car's lights. To a car driver looking in his review mirror, it would look as if another car were coming up behind him. As we got close to the vehicle in front of us, one of us would split off and go to the left side of the car and the other to the right. This move would startle the driver, as he saw headlights split and then heard a huge roar, while we went by.

During the day we would go to the mountains where there were steep dirt races. This was a challenge: to line up at the bottom of the hill, rev the engine, and take off up the hill, with dirt flying everywhere. Sometimes the hills were so steep that we would get bucked off our bikes, but fortunately, due to all the soft dirt, we had no injuries.

One weekend I headed to Saskatchewan to visit my girlfriend on her parents' farm. It was fall weather in Alberta—very cold—so I put newspapers in front of my legs under my pants to keep my legs warm. It began to rain, and the pavement ended as I turned onto a side road. The road soon became a "gumbo" (sticky, thick, slippery dirt) in which it is almost impossible to stay upright on a motorcycle. I soon found myself sliding down the road on my behind, to the rear of the motorcycle.

It was getting dark and soon a car came along. The driver understood my dilemma. The rain was slowing, and he said, "I will drive slow, and you follow in my car tracks, and we will soon be on a gravel road." What a relief! It worked, and soon I was on paved road again.

I soon discovered that if I got up on railroad tracks, up to fifty or sixty miles per hour, the railroad ties provided a fairly smooth ride. At slower speeds, it was teeth chattering. The hazard on the tracks came when there was a cattle crossing, because guards or grids were placed so that cattle could walk over them without getting their legs stuck between the guard boards or pipes. This meant that I had to stop and work my way around the crossing, then get back on the railroad ties. But even that was better than gumbo or loose gravel.

One summer evening my friends and I went to downtown Edmonton to go bowling. I parked my motorcycle in the bowling parking lot and locked the steering. We had a fun time, but when it was time to go back home, I walked to the parking lot to get my motorcycle—and it was not there! This seemed very strange, as I was sure I knew where I had parked my bike. I then realized that it had been stolen.

It's a strange feeling to have someone steal your property. I called the police, and they came and filled out a report. The motorcycle was never found.

> It's a strange feeling to have someone steal your property.

God was watching out for me. I had already planned to sell the motorcycle in the near future, so that I could go to university and advance my education. I had had it financed, and two payments remained. I didn't realize that financing included lost or stolen property. I was able to get a very good price for the motorcycle; more than I could sell it for by myself. If it had been stolen two months later, I would have been penniless.

☙❧☙❧☙❧☙❧

I thank God for His provision and timing and especially the protection that He gave me with all my crazy motorcycle episodes. I surely have a lot to be thankful for to God. And I'm sure you do, too. "Give thanks to the Lord, for he is good; his love endures forever" (1 Chron. 16:34, NIV).

Poisoned

Many years ago I was working the midnight shift at the University of Alberta Hospital in Canada and rooming with my good friends, Norman and Mary. Working the midnight shift meant I had lots of time in the day to visit friends and to enjoy recreational activities. One day I went down to a local gas station to visit two friends who were working at the service center.

At the center there were two service bays with hydraulic lifts to raise the cars for oil changes and other work. One bay was empty, so I walked over and stood on the lift. My friend promptly hit the lever, and up in the air I went until my head was not far from the ceiling. But then he wouldn't let me down. My friends thought it was a fun prank to leave me stranded up there. It *was* funny, at least at first.

> My friends thought it was a fun prank to leave me stranded up there. It was funny, at least at first.

However, because cars had recently been serviced, and their engines had been running in the center, carbon monoxide had risen to the ceiling. There was no air circulation there, either. I began to feel a little lightheaded and wanted to come down.

Fun time was over, so my friend hit the hydraulic down lever. You could hear the air escaping as it let me down. I was very dizzy now and staggered out of the bay into my car with only one thought in mind: to get to my rooming house and climb in bed. My friends thought I was just being goofy and waved goodbye.

I can remember veering from one side of the road to the other: that's how out of it I had become. But somehow I got to my rooming house, went upstairs, and climbed in bed. I was due to go to work at 11:00 p.m. that night but never made it.

The next morning Mary thought that something was strange, because she had not heard me go to work, and my car was still in the driveway. She became concerned, because I never missed work. She came upstairs and knocked on my door. I didn't answer.

Now she was *really* concerned. She opened the door and found me looking a cherry red color and sleeping. She tried to wake me up and found me very drowsy and slightly disoriented.

Mary took me to the hospital emergency room where I was found to have a toxic level of carbon monoxide in my blood. I was treated and made a good recovery. Somehow, even before the diagnosis, I knew I had been poisoned at the service station.

Today car and truck service areas are well-ventilated, and hoses are attached to the vehicles' mufflers to prevent the escape of carbon monoxide into the air that people breathe in the bays. That day I was so thankful for Mary's care, and for God saving me from a carbon monoxide poisoning death, which can happen.

༺༻༺༻༺༻༺༻

Carbon monoxide poisoning is very subtle. It reminds me how subtle the devil can be. We can be buzzing along in life, looking cherry red, but inside death and destruction will come if we are not following Jesus closely each day.

You know another thing? It is nice to have fun. After all, who doesn't like to do innocent pranks with their friends? We all do. However, we must always be careful, because we can't always foresee the outcome. I know that my friends would have never done what they did if they knew that it would make me sick. Thus, it's smart to make sure your jokes or pranks never hurt anyone.

The Cherry Bomb Blast in a Dorm Hall!

When I first attended Andrews University, I was living in the boys' dorm on the main floor, and my roommate was Dennis Gibbs, a pre-med major. We were great friends.

Christmas break came, and Dennis left for home, but I couldn't afford to go back to Canada to see my parents because I had to work my way through school.

"Have a good Christmas," Dennis said. "I'll be back soon."

Vacations always seemed too short, and when Dennis returned after his vacation, he did so with a surprise: a cherry bomb (which is like a huge firecracker that sounds like a bomb when it explodes)!

"Wow," I said. "Give it to me, Dennis."

He quickly warned me, "If you light it in this old, wooden dorm, it could catch fire, and we both would be out of here forever."

> When Dennis returned after his vacation, he did so with a surprise: a cherry bomb

Not heeding his warning, I found some matches, opened our dorm room door, lit the fuse, and swung the cherry bomb down the hall on the tile floor, as if I were throwing a bowling ball.

The cherry bomb stopped right in front of the dean's door.

Boom! Smoke and fire were everywhere. There probably weren't two cockroaches left in the whole dormitory after that explosion. I quickly closed our door, crawled under the bed, and hid behind the suitcases, leaving Dennis standing in the middle of the room.

The dean came flying out of his office. He had a very sensitive proboscis (nose) and figured out which end of the hall the cherry bomb had come from. As he got to our room, he could smell the fuse ignition fumes and knocked on our door. Dennis opened it, and the dean said, "Dennis, do you realize you could've burned down this dorm?"

"No, dean, I didn't do anything," Dennis said.

"Dennis, I will give you five minutes to get down to my office and confess, or you can pack your bags and be gone."

With that, the dean closed the door and walked back to his office. I started laughing and crawled out from under the bed. Dennis wasn't laughing.

"Dennis," I said, "you are my friend. I can't let you take this rap for me. I will go down and confess to the dean."

Realizing my freshman year at Andrews University was going to be a very short one, I walked down the hall to the dean's door and knocked. When he said, "Come in," I entered and got right to the point.

"Dean," I said, "I was the one that lit the cherry bomb, not Dennis."

"But I didn't see you in the room," he replied.

"I was hiding under the bed."

"You know the rules," he continued, solemnly. "You could be expelled for this."

"Yes, dean," I said, truly contrite. "I am sorry."

Then to my relief, he said, "Because you are man enough to come and confess, let's say this thing never happened. Forget what you did, but if you ever make another mistake like that, you can plan on packing your suitcase and being gone."

"Wow, thank you, Dean," I said, so relieved. "I won't disappoint you."

The dean put his trust in me, and so I was not going to let him down. What he saw in me, that he would give me a second chance after I did something so stupid, I will never know, But I had the highest respect for him from then on.

                                 ࿐࿐࿐࿐

He showed me mercy, not justice, and that is exactly what Jesus has done for me also. "For I will be merciful to their unrighteousness, and their sins and their lawless deeds I will remember no more" (Heb. 8:12). Yes, when we accept Jesus, no matter what we have done, even something as bad as what I did, He will be merciful to us, and even better He will not even remember the wrong things that we have done.

Graveyard Engagement

In 1963 I left my work with the Canadian Department of Health and Welfare in the Canadian Arctic and Yukon to attend Andrews University in Berrien Springs, Michigan. I drove from British Columbia to Andrews and began my education as a Physical Education major with a minor in Biology and Industrial Arts.

When first entering the P.E. building where registration was taking place, I was greeted by a pretty, senior physical education major who was assisting with the registration. I thought that I should get to know this lovely coed, but I was shy; it took a couple of months to ask Carol for a date.

University social restrictions then were so different from today. You were not allowed to hold hands. At chapels boys had to sit on one side, girls on the other. These social restrictions made dating a challenge, but one could be innovative in the name of love.

Our dates became more frequent, and soon we were thinking that life together might be just what God had planned for us. We had pastoral premarital counseling which gave us more confirmation that we were right for each other.

I lived off-campus boarding with the Lyzanchuk family, the owner/operators of Tri-Sum Bakery, located across US-31 from Andrews University. I would get up every morning and start baking at 5:00 a.m. After the sprouted wheat bread and other bakery goods were done and had filled the bakery with wonderful smells (that I remember so well, even to this day) I would head to class. Carol, meanwhile, resided with her girlfriends in a small, renovated house for seniors on campus. This was not like the big Lamson Hall dormitory where most girls resided and where it was much more difficult to sneak out.

Spring was on its way; crocuses and daffodils were popping out on the campus, and love hormones were flowing in the students as well. I had been dating Carol for four months and thought it was time to pop the big question.

One evening just after the sun had set, I thought it was the perfect time to sneak back onto campus and invite Carol for a car ride. We drove down US 31 to the stoplight in Berrien Springs, and then turned toward Rosehill Cemetery. Carol wondered why was I taking her at night to a *graveyard!*

I drove to a spot where there was a little hollow, and the roof of the car was at about the level of the ground, with the gravestones towering above. It was very secluded, quiet, and empty except for us and the sleeping dead nearby.

I turned the car lights off, and in each other's arms, I mustered up all my courage and asked if she would marry me. My heart was ticking so fast, but when she said "Yes!", the pounding stopped.

But she immediately asked, "Why did you pick a graveyard to propose?"

It was, I responded, a good place to start life together, because we would ultimately end up in a cemetery together as well. Besides, not every girl could boast that she got engaged in a graveyard!

༄༅༄༅༄༅༄༅

God has blessed us with fifty-seven years of marriage. Life has had joys and sorrows, but God has always been with us.

We were able to adopt our daughter Carmen, who was near death with infections and malnutrition, from Honduras. Decades later she and her husband, Craig, brought three lovely, little girls into our life. Our two other sons, Mark and Jeff, with their lovely wives, Chana and Jessica, have added eight more wonderful grandchildren.

But it wasn't all paradise. Our eight-year-old son David was riding his bicycle by our home when he was struck down by a drunk driver. I was able to resuscitate him, but his head trauma was so severe that he lived the next fifteen years in the silent world of a coma. We cared for him at home—the hardest thing in our lives—but we would not have had it any other way. David sleeps now. We can't wait for Jesus to burst open his coffin and place him in our arms for eternity along with our many other, sleeping loved ones.

༄༅༄༅༄༅༄༅

The most important engagement one can make in this life is with Jesus Christ. Propose to Him and give Him your heart, and He will give you His heart in return; an eternal heart of love. Jesus's love and commitment is forever, something that even the graveyard cannot break. You might slip and fall in your commitment from time to time, but He will always be there to pick you up.

And even if like our loved ones before us, we pass on before Christ returns, we have the promise of the resurrection ... *from the grave.* In that sense then, asking Carol to marry me and begin a new life together, in a graveyard, was more appropriate than one might think.

Why? Because it's from a graveyard, or wherever else the dead rest, that we will begin another, whole-new life together, only this time forever: "For the Lord himself will descend from heaven with a shout, with a voice of an archangel, and with the trumpet of God. And the dead in Christ will rise first ... And thus we shall always be with the Lord. Therefore comfort one another with these words" (1 Thess. 4:16-18).

Snake Stories

Midnight Visitor

I was working in a little medical clinic in the Honduran mountains. Tropical skin sores and parasite infections were among the most common ailments we treated. Others included wounds from machete cuts, hypertension, eye infections, malnutrition, and many other illnesses. The people were very grateful for help, and they seemed to enjoy prayer. However, many had no idea who Jesus was, even if they believed in a higher power or in powerful evil spirits (a common belief system in Honduras that is promoted by local witch doctors).

It had been a busy day of seeing patients, from babies to senior citizens. By sunset I was ready for a good night's sleep in the doctor's wood frame house. The inside was unfurnished. In my bedroom was a two by four bunkbed with open rafters above and not much else. Rain dropping rhythmically on the metal roof made for soothing sleep.

Around midnight I was suddenly awakened by something sliding off my head. I didn't feel any fur, claws, or scratches; nor did I hear any noise. I pulled my sleeping bag over my head and waited for some noise to let me know who the midnight intruder was. Finally, I fell asleep. The next morning at breakfast, I said to the doctor, "A strange thing happened to me last night. Something fell on my head and disappeared."

> *Around midnight I was suddenly awakened by something sliding off my head.*

He looked at me and laughed. The doctor said that some time ago, his son had caught a small boa constrictor down by the river, brought it home, and let it loose in the house. He said that it had grown to about ten feet in length. It crawled around the rafters at night, keeping the rats, mice, and other varmints away.

"So," he said, thinking to reassure me, "don't worry."

Well, I did worry. A ten-foot boa constrictor in my bed?

I didn't sleep well for many nights after that, preferring instead to stay well-tucked inside my sleeping bag.

Snakes are not all bad. Yes, some are poisonous and some constrictive (as in squeezing their prey to death), but most play a role in nature, like controlling the rats, mice, gophers, and other varmints. They also provide skin for clothing and shoes. Though before sin there was no death, now death plays an important role in nature. When Jesus comes, there will be no more death.

Desert Snake

While driving from Michigan to California with my wife, we had to cross the desert. We faced long stretches of flat highways with acres of sand on either side.

I saw something moving on the highway, and as I got close, I recognized a large rattlesnake slithering across the road. I slowed and watched the snake slide off onto the sand. I could see his large rattle tail and thought, *that would be a nice keepsake.*

I drove off the highway and followed him, catching up to him with my car and using my front tire to gently hold him stationary in the soft sand. Then I hopped out to check out the snake and his rattling rattle. I wanted to make sure he could not move enough to bite me, and I also wanted to ensure that I was not harming him while the car held him in place.

After admiring his cool colors, I got out my handy pocket knife and carefully cut his rattle off. I then jumped back in the car and backed up. I watched him slither away to grow some new rattles. When I lost sight of him, we got back on the road and continued our trip.

An interesting fact about rattlesnakes is that they shed their skins and form new rattle segments every one to four years. An amazing creation! And just as Jesus made the snake to regenerate its skin and rattles, so He will recreate us in new heavenly bodies one day soon!

Rabbit Snake

My brothers and I explored things in nature daily. We especially liked an area by a small lake near Victoria, British Colombia. Close to the lake sat a large, empty water reservoir. It had cement walls fifteen feet high and multiple compartments, each approximately sixty feet by 120 feet in size. There was another curved wall, sixty feet high, that created a huge cement arch. We could ride our bikes down the curved wall and up the other side. If we were not fast enough to get to the top, we would have to quickly turn, ride to the bottom, and push our bikes back up. It was a fun challenge.

One day one of my younger brothers, Jim, hit a rough spot by the cement wall and went flying over the handle bars, landing on his hands with outstretched arms. *Snap, snap!* Both wrists broke, and he had two floppy hands. PAIN! PAIN! PAIN!

We braced his fractures with newspaper and headed for home to get medical help. A doctor set his fractures and put both his arms in casts, and he healed well (in fact, he eventually became a dentist, which requires lots of hand and wrist activities, and he never had any problems).

Once Jim was healed we were back at the reservoir, riding the curve and investigating the bottom of the empty reservoir chamber. We saw a seven-foot snake with two huge bumps in his body. Curious as to what these big bumps were and noticing the snake was not moving well, we wanted to investigate. Looking at his round eyes, we were sure that he wasn't poisonous (slits or elliptical eyes could indicate a poisonous snake).

We decided that we needed to do surgery and find out what those large tumors, or bumps, were. Not wanting to cause the snake any additional distress, we popped his head with a big stick to knock him out. Then we got out our pocket knives and made careful incisions over the big bump. To our surprise, there were two rabbits! They were still looking good, but sadly they were dead. We felt bad for the little rabbits, but it was too late to save them. Looking back, I feel bad for the snake, too, when I think of the pain I caused this creature (even though it wasn't as cute as the rabbits).

I didn't realize it, but I was starting my medical surgical skills at very young age. Now I can put a person to sleep with a little injection, remove their bumps and lumps, sew them up, and (most importantly) wake them up. As a doctor, in a small way, I get to reflect the healing ministry of Jesus.

Gopher Snake

During my time at Canadian Union College, while I worked my way through school, a farmer in southern Alberta offered me a summer job driving a combine on his dairy and grain farm. We had wheat, rye, oats, and rapeseed to harvest. Riding up high in the cabin of that huge, new, Massey Ferguson combine was such a great job.

When the temperature and humidity were just right, you wanted to combine day and night to get the crops off and receive the most pay at the grainery without having to pay for drying expenses. It was a beautiful sight to watch the wheat in the night lights as it entered the combine.

Occasionally we would have a rainy day, which meant rock picking. It was hard work, and many of the rocks took two of us to lift onto the truck flatbed before driving over to the valley to dump them. The only fun part was watching them roll down into the valley below.

Off in the distance we could always see a shepherd herding his sheep. It reminded me of David, the shepherd boy long ago.

One day as I was combining, a snake about eight feet long showed up. Wow! What should I do with a big snake like that? I certainly didn't want him mixed in with the wheat! I stopped the combine and climbed down from the cab, taking a large hand shovel with me. It was a hot summer day, and the snake was moving very slowly. I thought I could sneak up on it and give it a big whack on the head with my shovel.

Just as I got close, it started to move towards me. I jumped back and brought the shovel down on his head, and then I quickly struck him again. The snake lay dead. Wow! I thought myself a hero, killing this huge snake.

> *One day as I was combining, a snake about eight feet long showed up.*

That evening at supper, I was telling my boss my hero story when I noticed the farmer was not amused. He said, "Gordon don't you ever do that again! That was a harmless gopher snake that crawls across my wheat fields eating the gophers that destroy my crops."

I did not feel like a hero anymore, and I apologized for my ignorance.

☙❧☙❧☙❧☙❧

So next time you see a snake, think what good it might be doing to help keep a balance in nature. Even in our fallen world, God uses various animals to preserve the environment for us.

A Heaven-Bound Astronaut (The Day Is Coming!)

In the late 1960s, I was working as a scientist in the physiology department for the Whirlpool Corporation. My responsibilities were to help design space food that the astronauts could use in space capsules and also to develop their waste management system. (As the old saying goes, "If something goes in the top end, something has to come out the bottom end.")

In the early years of space exploration, there were many challenges and unknowns. There had to be enough food for crew members for an entire space mission, while the volume and weight of the food had to be limited. There was no power for cooking or for refrigeration. The astronaut needed to be able to eat in a weightless state; thus, no crumbs or spillage could be allowed. The food system had to be able to withstand decompression and other rigors of space travel. Also, human waste needed to be dealt with effectively.

> *My responsibilities were to help design space food and their waste management system. (As the old saying goes, "If something goes in the top end, something has to come out the bottom end.")*

Because the design of the food products' packages was based on requirements for eating in the zero gravity stage, technicians developed a flexible container from which foods could be squeezed directly into the mouth. To eat freeze-dehydrated foods from zero gravity containers, hot or cold water was introduced. When finishing the meal, the astronaut would break a germicide pill into the package to retard the spoilage of food residue. The package was then placed in a waste storage space.

Bite-sized foods were also vacuum-packaged in plastic containers. Foods with a tendency to crumble were dipped in a special, starch-like substance that prevented crumbs while allowing astronauts to dissolve the bites in their mouths. A conventional meal of orange-grapefruit drink, beef with gravy, potato salad, chocolate pudding, chocolate brownies, and water was freeze-dried and packaged in special, flexible "spacesuits" to meet the problems of space travel.

Waste management systems presented their own challenges. A space diaper had to be designed as well as a urination container, so that no human wastes could contaminate the space capsule.

So one day I went downtown to the ladies' clothing store and picked out a few girdles. The sales clerk had a strange look on her face. When I said, "these are for the astronauts," she got an even stranger look.

Back I went to the research lab for experimentation. One of the staff was selected to put on a girdle, and peanut butter was used as a waste substitute. Once the peanut butter filled the girdle, the subject then had to jump, squat, walk, and bend or twist in many directions, in order to see if the "waste" was maintained in a secure position.

The astronauts did not like this space diaper, so we went on to develop a secure plastic bag with a Velcro ring that could attach securely to an astronaut's spacesuit. A special germicide pack was in the bag, and when the astronaut was finished eliminating his waste, the germicide pack could be broken to prevent any germ contamination. The bag was then placed in waste storage. A urination bag with an inflatable seal was also developed to be used during the elimination process. After use, it became secure for storage.

As progress has been made in the space program, we now have flush toilets; a great blessing to our male and female astronauts.

༺༻༺༻༺༻༺༻༺༻

I can't wait to be a heaven-bound astronaut headed through the opening of the constellation Orion at Christ's soon Second Coming!

"Save us, O Lord our God, and gather us from among the nations, that we may give thanks to your holy name and glory in Your praise" (Ps. 106:47, ESV).

"For the Lord himself will descend from heaven with a shout, with the voice of an archangel, and with the trumpet of God. And the dead in Christ will rise first. Then we who are alive and remain shall be caught up together with them in the clouds to meet the Lord in the air. And thus we shall always be with the Lord. Therefore comfort one another with these words" (1 Thess. 4:16-18).

One thing is for sure: we won't need any clumsy, human spacesuits then! We will be clothed in a heavenly astronaut spacesuit for eternity!

Gordon's Gin

Baseball season was in full swing in Kansas City, and the Chiefs were hitting hard. My six-year-old son, Mark, liked baseball and would collect baseball cards. He also knew all the players. One evening I surprised him by taking him to a Kansas City Chiefs ballgame. I think that he liked the popcorn, chips, and soda as much as the game!

I had a Ford station wagon, and in 1972 there were no seatbelt laws or airbags, so Mark was riding in the front passenger seat on the way home from the game.

We entered I-72 and headed to our home across from the Missouri River. Route I-72 was a four-lane highway, and I was driving in an inner lane. Just ahead, in an adjacent lane, was a small truck. I was traveling at seventy miles per hour when, suddenly, I saw something move in front of the truck. Not knowing if it was a person or an animal, I nevertheless just knew that it spelled danger.

The truck driver in front of me hit his brakes and began skidding. I was slowing down and passing him when—*bang*! Two people jumped in front of our car, and they both flew up in the air on impact. My son sat there stunned; speechless.

I came to a skidding stop, pulled the car onto the shoulder, and got out to examine the two bodies on the edge of the road. The couple's backpack had split open, and lying beside one of them was a bottle of Gordon's Gin. It seemed a little eerie that the alcohol bottle had my name on it.

They did serious damage to the front of my car, but fortunately, even amazingly, the impact didn't hurt them too badly: their backpacks took the brunt of the collision. Police arrived shortly, took pictures, recorded the accident scene, and the couple was taken away in an ambulance.

I soon received a court order to appear before a judge. The couple wanted to sue me for hitting them. *They ran in front of my car and they want to sue me?* I thought.

At court, the judge listened to the couple's arguments and then asked me a few questions as he looked at the police report. It was obvious that I had done nothing wrong and that they had no business running out in the road like that. Why would they have done something so reckless and dangerous? There was one answer: they were drunk. The bottle of gin was almost empty when the police found it, so the cops knew that they had been drinking and put that crucial fact in the police report.

The judge reprimanded the couple for being intoxicated and for jeopardizing the lives of others by running out into the road. He then told them that they had no suitable case. In fact, they were responsible for my car damage.

❧❦❧❦❧❦❧❦

The bottle might have had my name on it, but no bottle of alcohol is mine! Alcohol can be very addictive, and no one can know for sure whether or not they will become addicted after they drink it. Alcoholism is a terrible addiction and destroys not only the alcoholics but their families, friends, and others.

God's juice—water—is the best thing to drink. As the Bible says, "Wine is a mocker, strong drink is raging: and whosoever is deceived thereby is not wise" (Prov 20:1, KJV). Stay away from alcohol. It's a poison to the body and the mind.

Her Thirteenth Child

In my junior year of medical school, I had a one-month elective spot open. This was an opportunity to do special medical work. Wanting to do an overseas medical missionary ministry, I found a place in the mountains of Honduras: a small orphanage treating malnourished and abandoned children.

Children with all kinds of tropical diseases flowed to the clinic. Severe malnutrition, dehydration causing skin like putty, rotten feet with abscesses, wounds, all sorts of parasitic infestations, with worms coming out of every body opening and through the skin ... this is what we encountered there, and more. And it was all so heartbreaking.

I remember well a nine-year-old boy brought to the clinic by what I called a "Honduran ambulance." This was a blanket slung over a long wooden pole with one man at one end, another man at the other, and the person in need in the blanket. They had lugged this boy down mountain passages to the clinic where I was working. He had become very sick; malnourished and full of infections. Large, filthy dressings were attached with string to his arms, and he was unconscious. The lad's temperature was an outrageous 109 degrees Fahrenheit. This kills people, because the brain tissue itself is being destroyed at this temperature.

His mother had had thirteen children. All were dead but this one boy who, unless something was done quickly, would become her thirteenth dead child. Her hope was that our clinic could help.

There were no Christian doctors in her village but rather only witch doctors, whom the people trusted. They had to trust them to treat their sicknesses because, up there in the isolated mountains, they had no other options for medical care for miles around.

The witch doctor had made poultices of oils, witch brew, and scrambled eggs which he applied to the boy's skin (and this was supposed to help him?). Sadly, his condition worsened, and as a last resort, someone in the village told the mother to bring her son to our clinic.

His veins had all collapsed from fever and dehydration, so we placed the needles in his upper leg tissues for hydration and medicine. We did everything that we could ...

... But to no avail. He became number thirteen.

If only he had come to us sooner, I think we could have saved him. But the mother did not know that there were Christian doctors at this clinic who would use modern medicine and not witch doctor quackery. How sad to say goodbye to the mother and to send her back to the village, now bereaved of all her babies. Thirteen children, all in their graves! How much sorrow, sadness, and heartache can a mother withstand? It's a tough world, isn't it?

ॐ∽ॐ∽ॐ∽ॐ∽

That's why Jesus is our only hope. He is coming to raise the little ones who never had a chance to know Him. What a hope this offers to us all!

Does a story like this mean the devil wins and God loses? On the surface, yes; to those who don't know God, yes; for those who don't understand the great controversy, yes. But in reality, there is a final judgment coming, when evil, the devil, and even the witch doctors who con and deceive will one day receive their due reward.

The devil and unrepentant evil-doers will one day be forever gone, and God and those whom He has redeemed will be the ultimate winners. "And God will wipe away every tear from their eyes; there shall be no more death, nor sorrow, nor crying. There shall be no more pain, for the former things have passed away" (Rev. 21:4).

As a doctor who has seen so much pain, death, sorrow, and crying, I love this promise.

David and the Rattlesnake

Springtime in Okanagan Valley with its fruit tree blossoms created a feast for our eyes. My wife, two children, and I had driven to Canada to visit my parents, who were living in an apple orchard.

It was a beautiful piece of land with a river running along the bottom of the property. The river banks were made up of large, granite rocks, and you could walk or jump along them. The orchard was just one of the most beautiful and peaceful places that I have ever seen: a powerful revelation of God's love for us, to have given us such a beautiful planet, even after all the years of sin.

One warm day during our visit, my whole family decided to go for a walk along the river. Our oldest son, Mark, was leading the way, followed by my wife, then our youngest son, David. I was the last one in the line, keeping a watchful eye on my spouse and brood.

> Suddenly, I heard a noise that I didn't want to hear: a sharp rattling.

On this sunny day, chipmunks popped up between the rocks, and turtles and snakes were sunning themselves on larger stones. It was just so nice; so pleasant. You can feel close to God in nature.

Growing up in the country, I had learned to listen to the sounds of nature: wild animals, birds singing, squirrels chirping, insects buzzing, crickets chirping, and cicadas making their love calls. If you listened, you could hear a symphony, the conductor of which was God.

Suddenly, I heard a noise that I didn't want to hear: a sharp rattling. I knew that we were in rattlesnake territory, and one was giving me a message: "You are in my territory. Get out, or I will strike you." Wow!

The rattlesnake was curled up and wagging his tail, ready to strike David's leg. I quickly reached forward, grabbed a handful of David's hair, and lifted him straight up in the air—just as the rattlesnake struck at him, right under his shoe! It was such a close call.

The rattlesnake quickly slid off the rocks and was gone. We had escaped. And we moved on, a bit shaken but thankful to Jesus for protecting David from a serious bite.

                      ಌ⋙ಌ⋙ಌ⋙ಌ⋙

I learned some lessons from this experience.

First, we live in a fallen world, Yes, God's creation is beautiful, but because of sin, there are dangers as well. Though God created everything perfect, evil has come in and damaged it. A rattlesnake is one example of what sin can do.

Second, we need to keep our eyes and ears open, especially to the leading of God in our lives. God has given us ears to hear; not only things around us but His still small voice guiding us each day to make the right decisions. As the Bible says, "'This is the way, walk in it,' Whenever you turn to the right hand Or whenever you turn to the left" (Isa. 30:21).

Third, I learned that we must always thank God, not only in times such as what happened with the rattlesnake, but even in times when we don't realize the ways God has protected us. Praising and thanking Jesus: that's the best way to live.

Tattoos and Red Roses

Picture this scene: a steamy, vaporous, summer day in Michigan and my office waiting room packed full of patients, some probably getting antsy at the wait, too. Then in came a man looking straight out of Hell's Angels: long, matted hair, scraggly beard, lacking Right Guard (left guard, too), bare chest and arms covered in obnoxious tattoos (crosses, skull and bones, and non-G-rated inscriptions). A large, leather wallet with a chain dangled of his pants pocket. A long, sheathed knife was latched to a thick motorcycle belt. His tattered blue jeans disappeared into motorcycle boots. On the back of his wide open leather vest, the words, "Born to Raise Hell" were sewn (probably by some "biker chick"). Not my typical patient, and his outrageous presence no doubt disturbed my typical ones.

> *Then in came a man looking straight out of Hell's Angels. Not my typical patient, and his outrageous presence no doubt disturbed my typical ones.*

When his turn came, the nurse led him to the exam room. She checked his height, weight, blood pressure, and temperature and then recorded his chief complaint. I picked up the chart from the door holder and entered. As a doctor, I learned a long ago to read my patients, and I could tell by the look on his face that he was worried.

He told me a bit of his story. He left home young. Unfortunately, he got into the kind of bad company who quickly introduced him to tobacco, alcohol, and illegal drugs ... lots of illegal drugs. He also now feared that he had an untreatable, contagious disease that would take his life.

After a thorough exam, I assured him that, in spite of his fears, better days were ahead. I didn't see any signs of what he thought that he had contracted. Relieved, he quickly relaxed and willingly, even enthusiastically, agreed to comply with my recommendations and to keep a follow-up appointment. We shook hands, he left, and as soon as my next patient entered, I forgot about him.

A few hours later, as I walked by the receptionist desk, I noticed a beautiful bouquet of red roses and said to my secretary, "What lady sent us flowers?" (because sending flowers is how many ladies often showed us their appreciation).

With a stunned look, she answered, "No lady sent you anything."

"Who, then?" I queried, looking at the red roses.

"These came," she said, "from that smelly, bare-chested, tattooed motorcyclist who came in earlier."

છાઅિછાઅિછાઅિછાઅિ

What a terrible and judgmental mistake I had made, and what a great lesson I had learned. Beneath the chest of every human being, no matter their outward appearance, is a warm, beating heart that needs not only to receive love, attention, and respect but to give them, too. We were created to love and to be loved. Jesus knew that, which is why He treated everyone kindly, even those whose outward appearances might have made my biker friend look good.

This incident reminded me of what one of my medical school professors had counseled many years earlier: "When you are called into the emergency room," he said to the class, "and come face to face with a smelly, stuporous alcoholic covered in vomitus and other body wastes, love him; because somewhere, at some time, there was a mother who loved him, and you should, too."

No matter how gross or unappealing the external wrappings before me, I need to look beyond all that; way beyond to the internal, beating heart, which so desperately needs the love of Jesus. Christ's command, "that you love one another as I have loved you" (John 15:12), remains for me the most important thing that I can do for my patients ... even those who smell and who are covered in tattoos, and who *don't* send me roses, either.

Unseen Hands

It was a cold, snowy, icy Michigan day as I left my medical office to drive home. Just a few yards from my office, a street led down a steep hill to the main county highway. I applied the brakes, but the car kept sliding faster and faster. There was no place to turn ... and with banks on each side of the road, I knew that if I slid out into the highway while a car was coming, there would be a terrible accident.

Just as I feared, I began to skid out, and a car was, indeed, coming ... and coming fast. I could only pray, "Jesus, please help me!"

> *I began to skid out, and a car was, indeed, coming ... and coming fast. I could only pray, "Jesus, please help me!"*

I kept sliding, but then a strange thing happened to me. I could feel hands—yes, *hands*—pushing my car back onto the side of the highway and out of the path of the oncoming car. That car came right alongside me, only about two feet away. It then quickly passed, and we both went down the hill together; my car right behind that one.

And we both were safe.

I slumped in my seat, exhausted from the stress. Unseen hands had spared my life. All I could do was pray, thank God, and praise Him for again being by my side. "Thank you, Jesus, for my guardian angel, unseen but always present," I uttered aloud. "Thank you!"

Psalm 46:1 then came to my mind: "God is our refuge and strength, an ever-present help in trouble" (NIV). And *was I ever* in trouble then. But to this day I remember what happened, and I praise His holy name.

A Noise in the Mountain Trees

Our son Mark was studying French in Cologne, France, and he invited my wife and I to come and visit him during his spring school break. We toured the surrounding countries—Germany, Austria, Switzerland—as well as France.

We were finishing an exciting day's tour through Austria and France. It was near sundown as we arrived at the top of the French mountain called Salève. Our son suggested that we bed down for the night in a rooming house on top of the mountain. He said he would drive the car down and stay in his dorm room and then, in the morning, come back up and pick us up. It sounded like a plan.

The rooming house had a small bedroom with a high bed and big, feather bed covers. There was no heat in the room, and so it was a very cold night on top of the mountain. We snuggled and cuddled to stay warm, but got colder and colder.

At 2:00 in the morning, freezing, I finally suggested to my wife that I should get up and get dressed, walk down the mountain, retrieve the car, and come back and get her. Then we would stay in the men's dorm. While not exactly thrilled about the prospect of walking down a cold mountain at night in France, I didn't want us to freeze on top of it, so off I went.

The mountain side was so steep it required the road to be built in a switchback fashion, with the pavement going back and forth like the letter Z. While walking in the frigid dark, I heard a rustling in the leaves. This was very scary, because in the night darkness, your mind plays all kind of tricks on you. I imagined a wild animal following me.

Worse, when I stopped walking, the noise stopped. When I started to walk again, I heard noises in the leaves again. I knew then that I was not imagining things: a wild animal was tracking me! Scared, I prayed for God's angels to protect me.

I started to walk again, and again the rustling in the leaves began. As a young boy growing up in the Canadian mountains, I learned not to run, as that would cause the mountain lions or other wild animals to start chasing you ... and you are not going to outrun them. Though there were no mountain lions in France that were not in the zoo, I still didn't know what was stalking me. So I continued to walk slowly.

> *I knew then that I was not imagining things: a wild animal was tracking me! Scared, I prayed for God's angels to protect me.*

Coming to one of the switchback turns, I walked to the far side of the roadway, knowing that this would make it very hard for the mystery animal to jump off the high side of the mountain and onto me. I was becoming so scared my goose bumps were riding piggyback! I could envision the creature landing on my back, knocking me to the ground, and scarfing me down for a midnight meal. I thought that in the morning, my wife and son would find only bloody clothes and bones. I did not see myself as David killing a lion (or whatever beast was on my trail) with my bare hands, either (see 1 Sam. 17:34-37)!

I continued to pray, when suddenly the noise in the leaves stopped. l listened and listened ... nothing. No more noises, no more rustling in the leaves. Though still nervous and not totally calm, I continued my walk down the mountain, found my son, and we drove back up to retrieve my shivering wife.

ॐ⊷ॐ⊷ॐ⊷ॐ⊷ॐ

What was following me and rustling the dark leaves? To this day I don't know, though the only possibility was a wild animal hot on my tail!

I thank God for His protection. Many Bible verses come to mind, but this one really fits: "The Angel of the Lord encamps all around those who fear Him, and delivers them" (Ps. 34:7). I truly felt delivered that night on the cold mountain in France.

Free Fall Fiasco (Almost)

In my early adulthood, I was always looking for adventure. It could be climbing a mountain, riding a snowmobile across open water, spelunking, scuba diving, zip lining, or jumping out of a perfectly good airplane. One time sport parachuting got my attention, and I was off to the airport to join a parachuting club.

My instructor was a World War II veteran who had survived many parachuting injuries. Very safety conscious, he taught me how to pack my own parachute. The emergency chutes, though, had to be packed by federally-licensed riggers, obviously for safety reasons. After all, if the first one didn't open, the reserve was your last hope. (Another interesting fact: the Federal Aviation Agency (FAA) requires that an emergency parachute be repacked every 180 days by the licensed rigger, even if no one has jumped with it.)

I could hardly wait for my first jump. It was to occur in Dowagiac, Michigan. Your first five jumps had to be static line jumps. This meant that you had to have a special line attached to the airplane and to your parachute itself. As you fell, the static line would get tight and instantly open the parachute for you. All you did was fall, which was easy enough. After those five jumps, if you did well, you could then free fall, meaning that after leaving the airplane, you pulled the rip cord and opened the parachute yourself.

I felt well-trained, and finally the day came for my first static line jump. I donned my main parachute and my emergency one and climbed into the little Cessna 172, which had its passenger door removed.

My jump master was next to me, and the static line was securely attached to the airplane. When we reached 3,000 feet, I was told to step out of the airplane, stand on the wing foot support, and hold onto the wing strut. This put me in a hunched forward position outside the airplane while also receiving the full prop wash (air from the propeller). Finally, when we were over the landing target, my jump master gave me the signal to simultaneously let go of the strut and jump off the footrest.

I was so nervous when he said jump that I let go of the wing strut but didn't jump off the footrest. The second I let go, the prop wash and air speed threw me into backward somersaults. I was totally disoriented and doing backflips faster than I ever had in gymnastics. Then there was a gentle poof as the parachute deployed, and I was jerked into an upright position in my parachute harness. Not exactly the most graceful of exits, yes; but the static line did its work, and I was fine. It was so beautiful and quiet as I hung so peacefully in the air and surveyed the landscape below, with its tiny people and Matchbox-sized cars.

I spotted the big X that I was to aim for, so I pulled the toggle line by my head to close one of the parachute openings. This let more air out of the other opening and allowed me to turn and head toward my landing target. It was a thrilling experience as I landed gently, rolled over, then came quickly up onto my feet while the parachute itself deflated. I had jumped out of a perfectly good airplane! It was so much fun that I was going to do it again.

> *It was so beautiful and quiet as I hung so peacefully in the air and surveyed the landscape below.*

Not all jumps, however, went as well. A few times later, the wind was stronger. After my parachute opened, I was blown off target and had to search for a safe landing site. The only open area was the I-94 Interstate, with tall fir trees on each the side of the highway ... not an inviting landing site. I didn't have many options, however, and thought that the best place for me to land was on the median between the east and westbound lanes.

I had just enough height to skim across an overpass and land on that grassy median. Needless to say, I slowed the traffic down and frightened a few drivers. But I am sure none were more frightened than I was.

For some reason, my wife gently encouraged me to sell my parachute and pick another sport, like golfing. I hated to tell her (but did) that more people die by lightning strikes each year on the golf course than they do from parachuting accidents. She wasn't convinced by my argument, but neither was I by hers ... for the time being. Free falling was just so invigorating. You jumped out of the airplane at 10,000 feet, spread your arms and legs, and flew like a bird to 3,000 feet. You then pulled your rip cord, deploying your chute and gently descending, landing on the ground slowly enough so you could go back and jump again.

A water jump sounded like another thriller, so off to the lake I went. A water landing meant a gentle splash touchdown, then a designated boat driver rescued you and also picked up your emergency parachute, chute, and flotation gear.

If the reserve parachute is not sealed but gets submerged in water, it has to be inspected and repacked, so I brought a special bag to seal it in before I hit the water. We climbed to 10,000 feet, which would allow for a nice free fall. At about 3,000 feet, after my main chute opened, I had to untie the emergency chute and seal it in the waterproof bag. Somehow things didn't go right, and as I released my emergency chute, I also released part of my main harness and slipped partially out of it. In other words, I was suspended a thousand feet above the water with one arm hanging over the chute harness. One wrong move and I could have fallen out of the harness completely!

> As I released my emergency chute, I also released part of my main harness and slipped partially out of it.

A 1,000-foot fall, even into water, would kill you just as easily as if you landed on the ground. I hung on for dear life, literally, and dropped my emergency chute to the lake below. Fortunately, I stayed in the harness all the way down into the water, with my chute falling on top of me as the boat arrived.

Hanging there with only a partial harness around me was one of the scariest episodes of my long life! I was so thankful to be alive. My chute, as it fell on me in the water, felt like my guardian angels had covered me with their saving wings.

After that experience I thought that maybe my wife did know best, and I sold my parachute. I decided that the risk of a lightning strike on a golf course was, indeed, a better alternative.

~~~~~~~~~

When I think about that day, Psalm 91:4 still comes to mind: "He shall cover you with His feathers, And under His wings you shall take refuge."

The Disappearing Snowmobile

Michigan winters with lots of snow provided great snowmobile sport activities. The state marked out many trails and graded them for smooth and safe riding. It was always fun to get together with friends to go riding and racing along those trails. Often we made our own, and sometimes we would get stuck in deep snow, then have to pull each other out.

In upper Michigan there was a large river that flowed into Houghton Lake. The lake froze to a good depth; cars could safely drive on it, which the ice fishermen liked. The frozen lake also provided many miles of open snow for snowmobilers and ice boat sailors. However, expansion cracks in the ice were a hazard and could cause devastating accidents if you were to hit one at high speeds. The river, on the other hand, never froze and thus presented a different challenge to cross with a snowmobile.

I bought a used Arctic Cat for two hundred dollars. I thought it would be safe to run it across the open river because, if it didn't work, it would not be too big a financial loss! My buddies thought I was a little crazy but were certainly up to watching me run the river. Thinking that my Arctic Cat might not get all away across, I tied a rope to its front bumper, just in case it was needed for retrieval purposes.

The trick was to get to a high speed so that you could stay on top of the water and reach the riverbank on the other side. I got some distance back and lined up my snowmobile. Then, taking a deep breath with throttle on full, I gunned it, moving as fast as the vehicle would go. However, just before reaching the river, I hit a large, hidden chunk of ice in the snow that threw me off

> *Taking a deep breath with throttle on full, I gunned it, moving as fast as the vehicle would go.*

my Arctic Cat, which itself kept going ... right into the middle of the river! Before our eyes it slowly disappeared under the water.

I was not hurt, for the snow cushioned my fall. My buddies stood there, laughing hysterically, as my jaunt across the river ended in complete failure. Once over the shock of it all, we snowmobiled back to our cabin, put a canoe in the bed of our pickup truck, and returned to the river. In we paddled, and with a long pontoon pole, I retrieved the rope that I had tied to the front bumper. With the rope in my hand, we went back to the shore and tied it to the truck trailer hitch. We then pulled the Arctic Cat out of its watery grave.

The engine, full of water, would not start. We took it to a store, and they gave me $400 for the snowmobile as part of a trade-in for another used one. I thought that for a $200 investment, that was not all bad. With my newer snowmobile, I was much more careful and able to run the river without any problems.

***

Sometimes in life we make investments that pay off, and sometimes they don't. I have found that if we invest in Jesus Christ's life insurance policy, it guarantees us life eternal, and that is worth more than any investment that one can make in this old world.

> If we invest in Jesus Christ's life insurance policy, it guarantees us life eternal, and that is worth more than any investment that one can make in this old world.

Nothing the world offers can even come close to what Jesus offered us: His life for ours. As Jesus Himself has said, "For what is a man profited, if he shall gain the whole world, and lose his own soul? or what shall a man give in exchange for his soul?" (Matt. 16:26).

Think about it.

No Brakes and the Bull Moose (and Other Northern Adventures)

My partner and I were working for the Canadian Department of Health and Welfare out of Edmonton. Our job was to obtain chest x-rays on every Indian from northern Alberta throughout the Yukon as far as Alaska. This was an endeavor to eliminate tuberculosis (TB) in the 1960s. The trip would take three months.

Jack and I were both trained x-ray technicians. We had a three-ton truck with a diesel electric generator in the back to power our portable equipment. We would enter the Indian reservations and meet with the Royal Canadian Mounted Police (RCMP), who were in charge of the territory and responsible for giving the Queen's treaty money to the Indians.

Then we would meet with the chief, who would arrange for the people to come for x-rays. The Indians would not receive the treaty money until their chest x-rays were done. If we found TB, the patient would be sent out to a hospital.

It was a pretty sight on the reservations: the colorful teepees, the salmon hanging on lines to dry along with various animal furs. At our first reservation, I asked the chief to teach me how to say, "Take a deep breath and hold it," in their language, so that I could obtain a good chest x-ray.

The Joking Chief

We set up our x-ray machine on the ground with a lead shield in place to protect us from the scatter radiation. The scattered radiation was so strong that we could see the bones in our hands on x-ray film, but in those days there were no devices to record that radiation (as far as we know, no harmful side effects occurred).

We started the diesel engine and powered up our machines. I called the Indian chief to step up. Hundreds of others were watching, knowing that they each would have their turn.

With the chief in front of the x-ray machine, I said, "Take a deep breath and hold it" in the Indian language. Or so I thought. The crowd burst out in laughter. Some were rolling on the ground. The chief stepped away from the machine, laughing. I asked what was so funny. With a big smile, he said that I had told him to go around the corner and pee.

> I said, "Take a deep breath and hold it" in the Indian language. Or so I thought. The crowd burst out in laughter.

It was a good joke, and I laughed along with the people. Soon they were our friends. The chief then taught me how to say, with the appropriate words, "Take a deep breath and hold it." The others came forward for their x-rays, and the RCMP handed them their treaty money. It was a long day at work, but we were very happy when the last person was x-rayed.

༺✦༻✦༺✦༻✦

Road Grader Mischief

The Indians helped us load up our equipment, and we headed up the Alaska Highway for our next stop. At times there was not a field or any other place to drive our truck off the highway. We would set up our equipment right on the road. In the 1960s there was little traffic on the Alaska Highway, and it was a narrow road with gravel and dirt and lots of potholes. In those days, everybody traveling that highway carried extra tires and gas.

One afternoon we came across two idle road graders (these were big machines used to help smooth out the highway) parked in the ditch alongside the road. This could mean some exciting adventure: we had never driven road graders before.

> One afternoon we came across two idle road graders. This could mean some exciting adventure

We quickly parked our truck as far off the road as we could for safety. How were we going to start one of these without a key? It turned out that no key was needed. We found the little gas engine and started it up, then transferred the power to the primary, diesel engine. That one fired up with a big puff of black smoke ascending skyward. Yippy!

We jumped off the running grader and onto the second one. We soon had two graders ready to go.

"Jack," I said, "you drive this one, and I will jump off and get on the first one, and then you can follow me onto the highway."

The highway was a mess and certainly needed grading. Down went the grader blades and we were in business. We soon discovered, however, that our grading "skills" were destroying the Alaska Highway rather than refurbishing it, so we decided to park and mosey on up the highway. We felt quite proud of ourselves for just managing to drive the graders, even though we really didn't help the road much.

Gold Rush Town

Lodging was scarce, and gas stations were few and far between. At night we often found graveyards, and there, between the gravestones, we rolled out our sleeping bags for the night. It was eerie to go to sleep amid tombstones, and with wind rustling in the trees. The tombstones had many epitaphs carved in the stone, some reflecting young children's deaths. It was a rough life in the Northern country, especially with little treatment for infections.

As we drove into Dawson City, evidence of the old gold rush days was all around. Abandoned gold dredges, country stores, hitching posts, and a mortuary still in use ... right across from the lynching gallows, with a rope still hanging! Cheating, stealing, and other crimes were dealt with swiftly and usually with a cord around your neck. I'm glad those days are now gone.

No Brakes and the Bull Moose

It was June 21st, the night when the sun doesn't set (this is the origin of the term, "the land of the midnight sun"). We had reached the place where the Klondike and Yukon rivers join near Dawson. We had to cross the Yukon by ferry boat to get over to Alaska, make a loop over the high Chilkost mountain pass, then come back down to the Alaska highway before finally entering Yukon Territory.

We didn't need headlights as we climbed up to the top of the pass. The road was narrow, and large rocks bordered each side of the highway. As we headed down the mountain road, the truck began to go faster and faster. I applied the brakes, but the pedal went to the floor.

I quickly tried to downshift, but we were going too fast to get to the lowest gear. The truck was rolling faster and faster—and then a large bull Moose wandered onto the highway, not too far ahead of us!

> The truck was rolling faster and faster—and then a large bull Moose wandered onto the highway.

This was not good. A big bull moose could destroy a truck. The truck was moving even faster now. There was nowhere to go but straight down. Fortunately the road *was* straight, and if we could reach the bottom, the truck would slow on the upgrade.

Except there was still the slow-moving moose in front of us!

The moose looked bigger by the second. His eyeballs looked the size of saucers. I blew the horn, and he slowly began to walk off the road just in time to miss the front of the truck, though his rear end hit the corner box behind my driver's door. With a big *wham*, the truck jerked into the ditch, but I pulled it back onto the center of the road.

I looked in the rear-view mirror in time to see the moose spin around and slowly move away. We both breathed a sigh of relief and thanked God for His protection. We slowed on the upgrade, put the truck in low gear, and stayed in low gear until we got to a service station to get our brakes fixed. That had been way too close for comfort!

※ ※ ※ ※ ※

Looking back, I once again can only thank the Lord for His protection. We all surely have stories where the Lord has protected us. How good to always remember those times and to be thankful for them. I know that I am.

> Looking back, I once again can only thank the Lord for His protection.

The Slipping Ladder

It was a Sunday in June, 2017, and I had my suitcases packed. I was to go on a medical evangelism mission to Mongolia the upcoming Wednesday. Today I was doing odd chores around the house, so that everything would be in order for my wife after I left.

The eaves on the house needed to be cleaned out. My wife advised me not to go up the ladder onto the roof, but I thought that I would just be very careful. I set my ladder securely and climbed up, leaf blower in hand. I cautiously worked my way along the eave from the front of the house to the back. I was quite proud of myself.

I had only one corner of the eave left to clean out, which had the downspout plugged. I carefully set my ladder up above the bush hedge and over the air conditioning unit. Then I climbed up twelve feet to the roof edge, and as I was about to step off the ladder onto the roof, the ladder slipped away. I came face down on top of the air conditioner, rolled off into the hedge bushes, then onto the ground.

My face was lacerated, my nose broken, and my left knee in terrible pain. I crawled out of the bushes onto the grass and lay still for a few minutes to survey my injuries. How I wish I had listened to my wife's advice!

I hobbled into the house. My wife took a look at my bleeding face, and I knew what she wanted to say—"I told you not to go up on the ladder!"—but she didn't. Instead, she remained silent and helped clean me up.

> *My face was lacerated, my nose broken, and my left knee in terrible pain.*

I prayed for healing so that I could go on my mission endeavor that Wednesday, and I asked God's forgiveness for my foolishness. On Monday I went to my orthopedic doctor, who examined my knee and took a CAT scan, confirming a torn meniscus.

I told him that I was leaving on Wednesday for a medical mission in Mongolia. He said, "You can't go, because you need surgery tomorrow."

I said, "I can't have surgery now. Please, put me in a brace, and when I return, I will call you."

Not pleased, he agreed and told me, on my return, to call his office for an appointment for surgery. Wednesday came, and with a brace and sore left knee, I flew to Mongolia, where I had a successful mission service. *Thank you, God!*

On arriving home I was able to bend the knee and walk with a limp, but otherwise, it was not too bad. Feeling better, I decided to hold off on surgery and continue my knee exercises. I felt a little twinge once in a while, but I could get up and down from my prayer position quite quickly.

I thank God each day for His healing powers and for preventing a much more serious injury. My wife's wise (unheeded) words remind me how important it is to follow Christ's words: it could mean the difference between life and death!

> I thank God each day for His healing powers.

In Jesus's trial for instance, Pilate's wife advised him, "have nothing to do with that just Man" (Matt. 27:19). However, Pilate's pride and worldly position meant more to him than his salvation. Tragically, his golden opportunity for salvation slipped away, and his fate was set.

I am so glad that God gives us warning signs and the freedom of choice. I pray each day for Him to help me make the right choices, so that my salvation can be secure. I am also so thankful that God is merciful and understanding of our shortcomings. Many wonderful texts come to mind, this one in particular: "You, Lord, are forgiving and good, abounding in love to all who call to you" (Ps. 86:5, NIV). How grateful we should be, too!

Mongolian Hospice House Call

In June, 2017, the It Is Written mission team was in Ulaanbaatar, Mongolia. A huge medical evangelism group was winding up a long series of missions in that country that had started about four years earlier.

One evening at Pastor John Bradshaw's last sermon at the Mongolian Cultural Center, our health educator, Enka, asked if I would make a house call for a non-SDA family. A twenty-nine-year-old mother was in the terminal stages of neck cancer. The family was requesting a medical visit ... and prayer.

I readily agreed and was accompanied by a nurse, Dolly Hocking, along with two Taiwanese nurses who were part of the team, and an interpreter. We arrived at a secured high-rise apartment in a very poor part of the city and made our way upstairs to the patient's apartment.

It was tragic seeing this young mother lying supine in bed, bleeding from her nose and with blood oozing out of large, grape-like, cancerous masses on both sides of her neck. Unable to tolerate chemotherapy, she had chosen no more treatments. She just wanted to be as comfortable as possible as she awaited the inevitable. Despite her wretched suffering, she had a beautiful smile and welcomed us.

I could sense that the family and the patient were hoping that I had some miracle cure. Of course, in and of myself, I didn't. As a doctor I only did what I could: a history and a limited physical exam. I then assured her that no further medical treatment was available, even if she were in the United States. But amid all this, I did have some good news for her.

> *She had chosen no more treatments. She just wanted to be as comfortable as possible as she awaited the inevitable.*

Just before I had left home for Mongolia and while I was packing my doctor bag, I had spotted a small New Testament Bible on a shelf in my room. Although my bag was crammed full, I had had the very strong urge to put it in my doctor bag, not knowing then just how important it was to become.

So that day in the woman's home, before we left, I gave her my six-minute salvation talk. I began by telling her how Jesus created the world in six days and rested on the seventh day, the Sabbath. He also created Adam and Eve as free, moral beings; the only way that they could truly love Him and each other. However, they sinned in the garden of Eden, and this sin unleashed all the evil and suffering in the world, including her suffering now.

But God sent His Son, Jesus, to forgive us our sins and to provide an eternal home for us, if we would only claim it for ourselves. "Just as He forgave the thief on the cross who had nothing to offer Him," I told her, "Jesus will forgive you of all your sins as well."

I then took the little New Testament Bible from my doctor bag and, after reading John 3:16, gave it to her. Each of the nurses and I signed it. I reassured her of Jesus's love and asked her if she would like to accept Jesus.

> *"I would like to accept Jesus into my heart," she said.*

"I would like to accept Jesus into my heart," she said ... in English.

The family gathered around the bedside and we prayed. After the prayer her three-year-old daughter climbed down from the bed and came over to me and, in perfect English, said, "Thank you, doctor, for coming and praying for my mom."

How special was that? That child's simple expression of gratitude brought tears to my eyes ... and I think to the eyes of my team as well.

I never expected to make a hospice call on a mission trip. Yet to have someone accept Jesus on their deathbed and to know that, though she would soon sleep, the next thing she will experience is the return of Jesus—that experience alone was payment in full for making the long trip.

Our lifespans on this are earth are short, especially in contrast to eternity. If we are secure with Jesus in our hearts each day, we have a guarantee of eternal life and can claim John 3:16: "For God so loved the world that He gave His only begotten Son, that whoever believes in Him should not perish but have everlasting life" ... just as this young mother did.

Bleeding, Bleeding, Bleeding

It was a Sunday, spring afternoon, and I was playing with my grandchildren. On Wednesday I was to depart for a medical missionary trip in Moldova.

I had been losing weight but felt well, and I didn't think there was any major problem. But that afternoon my intestines sent a message to my brain, saying, "you need to go to the bathroom." So I excused myself and went. When I finished, I smelled blood. As a nurse or doctor can tell you, once you have smelled blood, you never forget that odor. So I turned and looked. The toilet was full of dark and bright red blood.

Weight loss and bleeding? Could this be the big "C"—cancer?

I called my stomach doctor, and he said to come right away to the emergency room. I didn't want to alarm my wife and told her I needed to get checked. It can take many hours sometimes, so I said I would call her from the emergency room. She explained to our grandchildren that I had an emergency and had to leave fast.

> Weight loss and bleeding? Could this be the big "C" — cancer?

I prayed as I was driving over, "God, I have been following your health plan and I have a medical mission coming up in three days, for you. If you want me to go to Moldova, I am relying on you to stop the bleeding and heal me."

Once I was at the emergency room, the physician evaluated me and said I had lost quite a bit of blood and would have to be admitted for further tests and an early morning colonoscopy. This is a procedure where the anesthesiologists put some fluid in your veins that puts you to sleep, and then the doctor can slide his long, black tube (that looks like a friendly, black snake) into your intestines to see if there are any problems there.

My wife is my "prayer warrior," and it was very reassuring to know that she was praying for me. Still I was very concerned and was trying to let God carry my fear.

I finally got admitted at 2:00 a.m., and the nurse promptly arrived with a gallon of "go juice" to clean out my intestines. Yucky tasting, for sure. This is the most difficult part: the preparation which cleans out your intestines before the procedure. Every hour I would go to the bathroom and still blood, blood, and more blood. As a doctor, I knew: this was bad!

At 6:00 in the morning, I was taken by stretcher downstairs to the colonoscopy procedure room. The anesthesiologists put some medication in my intravenous line, and I was off to dreamland in seconds.

I quickly woke up after the procedure. The doctor looked surprised. He said that he could find no evidence of bleeding anywhere, but because of all the blood loss, he would keep me there overnight. "Every few hours," he said, "we will check your blood count to be sure that you don't lose more blood. If, in the morning, your blood count has stabilized, you can go home."

Thank you, Jesus, I thought, *for answering our prayers!*

Frequently during the night, they took a blood sample. In the morning the doctor arrived, still mystified. Where had the blood come from? But with no further bleeding, I could go home.

I told him it was an answer to prayer, and he just smiled, though he said that I should not leave so soon for Moldova, because the health care there was not so good. "If you have a problem over there," he said, "you might very well come home in a pine box!"

I thanked him for his care and assured him that if I had any more bleeding, I would be calling him!

It had stopped, though, and there were no more or signs of cancer, so the next day, Wednesday, I was off to Moldova as planned. God blessed my medical mission, and I had no further bleeding while there.

On arrival back home, I had an unexpected call from the doctor. He said that he wanted me to come back in, "so I can scope you from top to bottom."

"Doctor," I replied, "I have had no further problems."

He said that because I had lost so much blood and my bowel prep was very fast, he needed to be sure that he hadn't missed anything. I reluctantly went back, appreciating his concern and praying again for God's reassurance.

"I don't know where the bleeding came from," he said to me after the tests came back, "but you have a healthy intestinal tract, and I don't need to see you again unless you need me."

As a doctor I know that you don't just bleed like that for no reason, but whatever caused it, I was now healed.

❧❧❧❧❧

Thank you, Jesus. I am so happy that Jesus is still in the prayer-answering and healing business. I know that healing does not always come, but we can be especially thankful when it does, that's for sure!

A German Shepherd Puppy Opens Closed Government Doors in Mongolia

It was March, 2018, and an It Is Written medical mission trip to Erdenet, Mongolia, was in full swing. But suddenly, on March 19, we received word that a spy had revealed our medical work to the government and that, as a result, we were ordered to stop. What should we do? We had come prepared to provide medical care to the needy Mongolian people, and now we would have to *leave* before barely getting *started*? This just didn't seem right.

We united in prayer, asking the Lord to open up the closed door for His glory. A local Adventist pastor named Gantumur heard about our difficulty. He knew a government official, and he said that he would do whatever he could to help us.

Pastor Gantumur bred prized German shepherd dogs and had become friends with an official to whom he had sold a puppy. He called this friend and scheduled a meeting for 9:00 a.m. the next day at the Erdenet church.

Pastor Gantumur, along with Pastor Tumunuu, who led the Erdenet church, my interpreter, Uka, and I all met with this tall, impressive, and solemn government official.

At first, he asked specific questions about our work and about the medicines that we brought. We told him all about that, and we also explained that we were here to serve his people in any way that we could. Our only motive, our only reason to come was to be a blessing to anyone we could help.

He quickly responded and said, "You cannot see any more patients in the city."

Our spirits immediately began to sink, but then he continued.

"I will arrange instead," he said, "for you to see very poor people on the outskirts of town. Give me a few hours to make arrangements, and you can start seeing patients tomorrow morning." He then quickly arose and left.

We were momentarily stunned. God closed one door but opened up a new one where the need was even greater (God's ways are the only ways; we just need to be patient ... and to trust).

We saw the poorest of the poor on the outskirts of Erdenet, including a young teenage boy with a very visible congenital anomaly. When you find one anomaly you have to look for others, and it soon became evident that his concern, the anomaly that brought him to us in the first place, was minor compared to what else we found. He was in respiratory/heart failure, his oxygen saturations were low, and he had a heart murmur that you could hear without a stethoscope! We told his older brother about his heart problem and that this issue, even before his congenital anomaly, needed immediate attention. He was then referred to a hospital.

> We were momentarily stunned. God closed one door but opened up a new one where the need was even greater.

God knew that we were needed in the outskirts of Erdenet, and the hospital clinic staff was so appreciative of our services that they invited us back.

Thus our team was doubly blessed. We left Mongolia rejoicing with heavenly heartbeats for our God, who loves us so much and who answers our prayers. It truly was a blessing to be able to serve others and to do so with no expectation of anything in return other than the satisfaction of seeking to be, in our own feeble ways, representatives of Jesus.

༄༅༄༅༄༅༄༅

If a little, German shepherd puppy can open closed doors, just think what God can open for you and for me so we can serve Him better each day ... if we are willing. That is the key: to be willing.

Why not join an It Is Written medical/evangelistic team? Your life will be forever changed as you experience for yourself what it means to be like Jesus, as a medical missionary.

Do Angels Carry Suitcases? Mission in Moldova

On February 24, 2019, I was booked on my medical missionary flight from Atlanta to Moldova. I flew first to Paris but encountered a flight delay on the leg to Bucharest, Romania, meaning I would miss my final flight from Bucharest to Moldova.

When I arrived at Bucharest, my three fifty-pound suitcases, filled with all my medical and church supplies, were missing. I went to the luggage office for help. The lady took my luggage tickets and phoned Paris, confirming that my three suitcases were still there. I asked her if she would have them sent to me here, in Bucharest, and she said, "No, you will have to claim lost baggage at your destination, in Moldova."

I was praying. I had missed my Moldova flight, and now I had to go to the ticket counter and reschedule. I was the last in line, and the agent said the 8:00 a.m. and 10:00 a.m. flights were already full. I could take the 2:00 p.m. flight, though. I begged for an earlier flight, but he said there was no space. He phoned Paris again and confirmed my suitcases were still there.

I phoned Pastor Zaharia in Moldova, and told him I would not make my Sabbath appointments and that he should find a place for himself to stay that night. He and Pastor Adrian went to Pastor Zaharia's sister's residence, and there they filled a very needed preaching spot on Sabbath. In the end, it worked out for the best.

> Then I realized why God had not allowed me to buy tickets for an earlier flight.

Meanwhile I got to the hotel at 4:00 a.m. and then was right back to the airport at 10:00 a.m. to claim my three suitcases ... still in Paris. Then I found out the morning flights were cancelled and my 2:00 p.m. flight was delayed. But finally we departed. Then I realized why God had not allowed me to buy tickets for an earlier flight: I would have been stuck in Bucharest for days.

When finally, after delays, I got to Chisinau, Moldova, Pastors Zaharia and Adrian met me. Pastor Zaharia spoke Russian to the agent and told him my lost luggage was still in Paris. The tall, stoic agent (who spoke only Russian) asked for the baggage stubs, told the pastors to wait in the hall, and took me through the hallways to a luggage area. The carousel belt was running with no luggage on it.

He motioned to me to stand by the carousel, then disappeared though a door to the storage area. Suddenly, the wall luggage flaps separated and one of my suitcases appeared. To my astonishment, a second appeared, and then to my further amazement, out came the third.

I was dumbfounded! We had received no notice of the bags ever leaving Paris, but here they were! Did an angel carry my three suitcases over from Paris?

I know only that my prayers were answered.

Teaching, Preaching, Ministering

Our day started at 6:30 a.m. with Pastor Adrian's wife, Natalia, making us breakfast. Afterwards we traveled to the Drochia church to conduct medical examinations, followed by children's stories, health talks, and the sermon.

One of Pastor Adrian's church ladies was always looking to witness. She worked in a furniture factory where most of the workers smoked and where absenteeism was high because of alcohol abuse. She went to the owner and told him that a doctor from the United States was visiting her church and that he was doing health lectures on smoking and drugs. Would he be interested in us giving a lecture for his workers? she asked him. Her boss, excited, extended me an invitation.

The next day Pastor Zaharia, Pastor Adrian, and my interpreter accompanied me to the factory. To my surprise the factory owner shut down his plant production and had all his employees listen.

I presented a health talk on the heart and lungs and on how to stop smoking. I talked about alcoholism and the benefits of sobriety. The workers were attentive, thankful, and inquisitive. The owner, most grateful, invited me back. What a witness this church lady was for Jesus, the Great Healer of addictions.

The next day, after more medical exams in the church, we went to a government college in Riscani, and gave drug education presentations. Following these programs we moved to the Riscani SDA church for medical exams, children's stories, health talks, and preaching.

Pastor Zaharia and I usually ended up back at our hotel by 10:00 or 11:00 at night. On Thursday night we said goodbye to the Drochia and Riscani church families and drove to Pastor Zaharia's home church in Edinet.

Now in the Sofrincani area, Friday was another exciting day. At a high school, I spoke about drug abuse, and at the end of each lecture I would ask the students if they would like to see my best friend. I would show them the artist Nathan Green's picture of Jesus extending His hand in welcome. I would tell them that, whatever their belief, there is a higher power whom they could call on twenty-four seven. When asked if they would like to be drug-free, every hand went up.

> When asked if they would like to be drug-free, every hand went up.

Following the student dismissal, Pastor Zaharia, who never missed an opportunity to witness, invited the teachers to have physical exams, and they readily agreed. These people did not visit doctors often and seemed unaware of breast self-exams, hypertension, diabetes, or other health care needs. We found two diabetics, with one having a blood sugar over 500 (a normal high is 100)! Two ladies had palpable, abnormal breast tissue, and I sent them to get mammograms. I am amazed how God leads and brings people to us.

After these appointments we went to the Bratusani Church and met with the students there. The pastor taught English using the It Is Written children's Bible as his textbook. Most of these children were non-Adventists from my earlier Moldova vacation Bible school (which Pastor Zaharia, his wife Liliana, and my granddaughter Katie had conducted). The children led their parents to come, and so the door was opened for them to hear about salvation in Jesus. What a fantastic outreach.

On to Edinet we went for Friday evening vespers, then Sabbath services at Edinet and Hallahora.

At the Edinet Church, people were asked if they'd like to have health checkups on Sunday morning, and about half a dozen said yes. I figured that we'd have a short checkup in the morning. Little did I know that the members went home and called their friends, mostly non-Adventists, to come on Sunday morning.

With Pastor Zaharia's wife Liliana as my interpreter, we worked from 9:00 a.m. to 2:00 p.m. and saw about forty patients. The people were so grateful that they loaded me up with fruits, baked goods, preserves, and

Moldovan honey (the best honey in the world)! Sunday evening, Pastor Zaharia and I drove to Chisinau in preparation for an early morning flight back home.

◈◈◈◈◈

More Providences: God's Hands on Mine

I knew that my baggage was overweight and that the extra airline fee would be high. We walked into the hotel at 11:00 p.m. and met our team leader, Pastor Douglass Na'a, in the doorway. He agreed to take my extra luggage back home with him. Another one of God's blessings.

Reflecting on those blessings, I recalled an incident in the middle of my last sermon in Riscani. During the sermon I noticed when a mother and her fourteen-year-old daughter who were sitting in the back of the church abruptly walked out. The girl looked pale and in pain. I was quickly called to go upstairs to a room where I could examine her. I asked the pastor to put music on for the congregation and to say that I would be right back.

The girl was sweating from intense low back pain, and she could not bend forward or backward. I placed her on the examination table, examined her, and treated her back and hip area with manual medicine. I then asked her to stand up, and she said she had no pain and could bend backward and forward and touch her toes without pain. After seeing many doctors, she was pain-free for the first time in eighteen months.

Her mother was speechless, and her grandmother, with tears in her eyes, hugged me and kissed me on each cheek. We then returned to the church and continued the service.

Medicine has taught me many skills, and I know that Jesus had His hands on my mine as I treated this lovely young girl. Yes, Jesus is still in the healing business: physically, mentally, and spiritually.

The next day our It Is Written mission endeavor was over, but the work was just beginning for the Moldovan pastors who would follow up on our contacts.

> *Medicine has taught me many skills, and I know that Jesus had His hands on my mine as I treated this lovely young girl.*

◈◈◈◈◈

We serve an amazing God who loves us so much. I'm in awe at such an awesome God and the privilege He gives me to serve people for His glory, even in such faraway places as Moldova where every soul is close to Jesus's heart.

Miracle Worker

It was March of 2021 and a typical mission day in Costa Rica: hot, steamy, muggy. Workers were sweating away in the heat at the church building site; medical day clinics were helping as many as they could; workers' lunches were being prepared by church ladies with busy hands; plans for the evening children's programs, health talks, and sermons were all underway. Everyone was busy; very busy.

At night there were five evangelistic teams spread out at five house meetings. I went from site to site for the health education talks and for children's stories. One Tuesday evening I arrived at a humble, single story home when the evening sermon was just finishing. I was told that a lady sitting in a sofa-type chair needed medical help.

She had a facial droop, a limp left upper extremity, and a lack of left facial expressions. This did not look good at all ... and certainly was nothing that I, with a doctor's proverbial "black bag," could help with. I warned her seventeen-year-old daughter that her mom was having a stroke, and that she needed to go to the hospital as soon as possible (in other words immediately) for evaluation and a CAT scan.

The first seventy-two hours are crucial for stroke evaluations, because we need to deal with the blood clot as soon as possible before there is permanent damage. But the daughter was reluctant to take her forty-four-year-old mother to the hospital, because on prior occasions, they had simply given her a cursory examination and then, doing nothing, sent her home. Also, they did not have CAT available at the nearest hospital, meaning they would have to schedule the scan at another location and send her there.

I warned the daughter again that her mom's condition was very serious, and that we needed to act now. The daughter requested that I finish my health program and then reevaluate. Because I was in no position to force anything, I could only do my health talk (though you can be certain that I rushed it!). At the end, when I returned to the unfortunate woman in the chair, her symptoms were worse. There was more facial weakness and no speech at all.

Again, but with more urgency than before, I stressed that her mother needed medical care at the hospital *right away*. The daughter said that she would watch her mom, and if she got worse in the night, then she would take her to the hospital.

However much I disagreed, I had to prayerfully respect the daughter's position. What could I do? Medicine and how patients perceive their needs in foreign countries can be very different from the U.S. and Canada, and as a doctor you have to have patience and trust in God to guide you along.

So I could do nothing except, of course, pray. We gathered our team around the patient, laid our hands on this very sick woman, and prayed for God's healing. I must say that my faith here was being sorely, sorely, tested. We left feeling helpless and worried about the woman, even though we knew that God was the Great Healer and could perform a miracle. And from all I knew about medicine, this woman would need a miracle ... a big one!

> Medicine and how patients perceive their needs in foreign countries can be very different from the U.S. and Canada, and as a doctor you have to have patience and trust in God to guide you along.

The next morning I saw her daughter and, quite worried (and almost not wanting to know), I asked, "How is your mother?" I was thinking that I already knew the answer would be, "Not good."

Instead, smiling, she said that her mother was fine. Her face was normal, her left hand was fully functioning, and as we spoke, she was preparing our lunches. My heart jumped for joy and gratitude to a prayer-answering God.

As a medical doctor who had dealt with many stroke victims, I knew for certain that this was a miracle from God. Stroke victims don't just get well quickly on their own with no medical treatment. Then I remembered the story of Jesus healing the paralytic: "Rise, take up your bed and walk," He had said to the man. And what did the man do? "And immediately the man was made well, took up his bed, and walked" (John 5:8-9). This same Jesus was at work that day. Instead of taking up her bed, the woman took up her daily work of preparing meals for everyone there during the mission project. It was truly a miraculous healing.

෴෴෴෴෴

Though stories like this don't happen every day (believe me, as a doctor I know that), I have still seen enough to know that God cares about our health, and that the same Jesus who healed that paralytic is, indeed, at work today as well.

Siberia Mission Adventure

In 2020, It Is Written planned a medical evangelism outreach to three cities in Siberia. My suitcases were loaded with my medical supplies, and I boarded my Air France flight on March 11, at 9:15 p.m. The route would take me from Atlanta to Paris to Moscow to Omsk, in Siberia. I was to arrive on March 13.

The plane started to back out for taxiing, then it stopped. Some people heard on their cell phones that President Trump had stated that all European flights coming into the U.S. would be stopped at midnight on Friday, March 12. Thus, people were given the option to deplane if they chose.

Taxiing for take-off resumed, but I then got a text from my son and wife with same information: *Please get a return flight from Paris tomorrow morning, or you will be stuck in Europe until March 30.* In other words, as soon as you land in Paris, turn around and come home.

I prayed, "Jesus, this is your mission, not mine. I am only a servant in your hands. Please show me clearly what to do: return home from Paris, or continue onto Siberia. Amen."

God answered through my wife. When I arrived in Paris, her text message read, *President Trump misspoke. You will only be screened for the COVID-19 virus in order to reenter the USA.*

Thank you, God, I thought, *for answering my prayer!*

I was on my way to Moscow, from where I would proceed to Siberia. I arrived at 7:00 p.m. on March 12, five hours before my Russian visa for the 13th would become effective. No way was the border patrol going to let me through. All entries were computer controlled. Thus, I had to wait, and I missed my Omsk flight.

They rescheduled me for 12:15 a.m. on the 13th, but then they told me that I would never be able to navigate the stairs, elevators, and bus awaiting me between my two terminals within the allotted fifteen minutes. They wanted to reschedule me again, for a 7:00 a.m. flight. I said, "Let me try for the 12:15, anyway." While I waited, I tried three different passport control personnel, but had no luck.

I entered passport control at 12:03 a.m. I went through, then put on my seventy-eight-year-old "traffic running legs." With my roller bag behind me, I said, "God, I need my guardian angel to help me fly through this airport to Terminal B, which is miles away."

I began. Down the hallway, down an escalator, a 180 degree turn down another escalator, a hallway run, through another upstairs hallway, flying past a moving conveyor belt, into an elevator up three floors, then out the door into a bus, just as it was ready to leave. Then out of the bus, up the escalator, and into an open shopping area.

There was an arrow for Terminal B. I took a shortcut through clothing stores, a perfume shop, and a lingerie boutique. I came to a departure sign in Russian which I could not read, but a gentleman saw my need and pointed to a girl behind the counter. I ran over and asked, "Can you tell me the gate number for Omsk?"

"It is number seven," she said, "but you are late, so you better run fast."

I'm sure my heart rate was 160 as I ran down the hall and though an empty gate area. An agent appeared and processed my ticket, and I ran down the gangway just as the airplane door was closing. I barely made it through and dropped into my seat: the first row behind first class.

That was a cardiovascular test, for sure. I prayed, *Thank you, God and my guardian angel.*

The Meetings

Pastor Sergey had come to Omsk airport at 4:30 a.m. for me and my partner, Airforce Colonel Tom Steinbrenner. He had made his flight, so only he showed up. They had no idea where I was.

I arrived in Omsk at 7:30 and called Pastor Sergey.

"I will be there," he said, happy to hear my voice, "in fifteen minutes."

He soon welcomed me with a nice, Siberian hug. We dropped off my luggage at the very secure Hi Loft hotel and went directly to the church in order to set up the medical clinic. Our evangelistic program began that evening with wonderful music, a children's story, a health talk, and a sermon.

We had gourmet food every afternoon and evening, for the church ladies made sure we had lots of nutritious supplementation. Pastor

Sergey brought us breakfast food at the hotel, and every morning Colonel Steinbrenner would gather the food, go downstairs to the kitchen, and prepare special, fruit-oatmeal cereal with sliced apples and pomegranate kernels, which are rich in vitamin C, potassium, and fiber (fiber gives you floaters not sinkers, which is very healthy for you). What a great roommate!

We were missing our group leader, Pastor Yves Monnier, and our sermon leader, Sandy Firestone. Both had arrived in Moscow but were advised to immediately return home due to the COVID crisis and border closings. Thus, Tom pitched in and helped me with sermons, children's stories, and health talks. God always provides. Our daily schedule was a 9:00 a.m. to 2:00 p.m. medical clinic in the church, home visits, and the evening meetings. One afternoon Pastor Sergey and Igor, one of our translators, gave us a city history tour which we found fascinating.

> God always provides.

In my morning medical clinics, I had two excellent translators. Anna helped with the ladies' exams. President Vasili had sent her from one of the conference offices which was about an eight- to ten-hour train ride away. How thoughtful of him, and we so appreciated her. Though Anna was not medically-oriented at the start, she certainly was when she left. Plus she was a Spirit-filled gift to us and a delight to work with.

Igor was an English tutor. He understood my Canadian fast talk and was outstanding in translations, both in the clinic and in the evening messages.

Pastor Sergey had scheduled the patients in such a way as to give us time to examine, counsel, and do blood sugar checks if needed. Pastor and Mrs. Mikhail got to hear the *thump, thump, thump,* 146 beats per minute of their little unborn boy, Elijah. After delivering over 1,000 babies, I am still thrilled to listen to fetal heart tones. That rhythm is God's music for an upcoming miracle.

Throughout the medical exams, it became evident Omsk had great, free medical care, but the patients had little understanding of their health-related problems or that their lifestyles needed changes. There were many musculoskeletal issues among the people, so osteopathic manipulative therapy (manual medicine) was applied. One lady came every day for manual medicine followed by massage therapy for her severe neck pain. One of the church ladies and Pastor Mikhail offered excellent treatments.

At the end of each exam, the patients welcomed prayer, as we held hands and shoulders. Some of the patients then prayed for me and our mission team. How sweet was that!

We did eye exams and gave glasses if needed. Then we sent patients off to see my "pharmacist," Tom, who had sorted and packaged all my nutritional supplements. The old Colonel learned fast! Tom and the pastor checked the patients' BMI, did strength tests, gave lifestyle counsel, and held spiritual enrichment and baptismal classes. This program rounded out It Is Written's approach in seeking to follow Jesus' example: treat physical, emotional, and spiritual needs as you make new friends for Christ.

> How privileged we were to be part of Jesus's commission, "to go into all the world and preach the gospel" (Mark 16:15).

Three baptisms resulted, with more to come. This number may seem small compared to a few hundred in India or Africa, but it was a major breakthrough in the Russian spiritual environment. How privileged we were to be part of Jesus's commission, "to go into all the world and preach the gospel" (Mark 16:15).

Our talks and demonstrations about God's natural health remedies sparked much interest. I had set up the massage table on the church platform and demonstrated manual medicine treatments for upper and lower respiratory problems, as well as hydrotherapy for sinus/head congestion and colds. Pastor Mikhail and his daughter were my volunteer patients. The next evening church members asked if we could repeat the program, so we brought the table back up and reviewed it all with them. The people were so precious, loving, and appreciative.

All through the week we were advised to come home as soon as possible, as COVID was causing border closings and lockdowns everywhere. But how could we not complete our mission? We prayed for God to keep the church doors open until our last Saturday meeting, and He did.

The whole city of Omsk was quarantined shortly after we left. I was scheduled to go to Romania next, in order to help a new, young pastor open a new church. But Romania had closed all churches and social gatherings, and was cancelling flights and imposing quarantines, so I had to cancel my mission there and change my route to home.

Fortunately, my travel agency, Butler, was able to get me one of the last flights out of Moscow, to JFK in New York. I was able to pass the COVID-19 screening and flew on to Atlanta. My wife, my prayer warrior, picked me up at the airport and gave me a big, American hug and kiss! It was good to be safely home.

☙❧☙❧☙❧☙❧

God delivered me from Siberia just as He delivered the children of Israel from Egypt. And He is still in delivery mode for everyone's spiritual life. I thank God each day for His watch over us. Satan is closing many doors, but God is opening many more, and His message to a dying world cannot be stopped.

TEACH Services, Inc.
P U B L I S H I N G

We invite you to view the complete
selection of titles we publish at:
www.TEACHServices.com

We encourage you to write us
with your thoughts about this,
or any other book we publish at:
info@TEACHServices.com

TEACH Services' titles may be purchased in
bulk quantities for educational, fund-raising,
business, or promotional use.
bulksales@TEACHServices.com

Finally, if you are interested in seeing
your own book in print, please contact us at:
publishing@TEACHServices.com
We are happy to review your manuscript at no charge.

www.ingramcontent.com/pod-product-compliance
Lightning Source LLC
Chambersburg PA
CBHW070541170426
43200CB00011B/2499

Praise for *The Adventures of Freckles: Life Lessons from a Mischievous Son of Canada*

Autobiographical Sketches by Dr. Gordon Guild

"When I think of Dr. Gordon Guild, I think of Colossians 3:23: "Whatever you do, do it with all your heart." This wonderful collection has stories of Dr. Guild living and working with all his heart—from medical missions in Mongolia and Honduras, to snowmobiling across the river ice, to releasing squawking chickens in the girls' dorm. Truly Dr. Guild has lived life to the fullest—and as a child of God, he's only just begun."

—Andy Nash, Ph.D., Pastor and Professor,
Southern Adventist University

"Fun and interesting stories that will keep you on the edge of your seat! Fun to read, but I don't recommend trying any of his pranks at home!"

—Lauren, High School Student, age 16

"I love the adventures and spiritually uplifting stories written by Dr. Guild. Parents and all readers will be blessed by his Christian values that lead us to Jesus. This is a book every family and church worker should have in their library."

—Dr. William D. Fisher DO, ACOFP

"Delightful, exciting, true-life stories with solid moral lessons. What mother can't identify with such mischievousness? Follow the journey of a small-town Canadian kid from his childhood experiences to those as a Mission Doctor. These stories will thrill children and adults alike—a *must read* for all ages!"

—Chana, Homeschooling Mother of 5

"Dr. Guild's book is an amazing compilation of children's sermons that may be used to bless children and adults everywhere. Each story contains Scripture verse applications and Bible principles that teach lessons of God's love and majesty. This is an amazing resource for pastors to use when searching for sermon illustrations. It is an asset to anyone serving in Children's Ministries. In addition, it is a gift to any parent or grandparent who desires to touch their children's hearts for Jesus."
—Carole Verrill, Children's Pastor of the Collegedale Church

"Children love to hear stories told by Dr. Guild. He has given his life to serve as a physician and missionary. As a result, he personally has experienced the love and power of God. These experiences are shared in this book to testify to the fact that the Lord continues to be active in the lives of His people. I highly recommend this book for children, families, and all those who want to be reminded about the limitless power of our God."
—Dr. Kris R. Eckenroth, D.Min.,
Speaker/Executive Director Retro Ministries